making garden floors

making garden floors

STONE, BRICK, TILE, CONCRETE, ORNAMENTAL GRAVEL, RECYCLED MATERIALS, AND MORE

Paige Gilchrist

LARK BOOKS

A Division of Sterling Publishing Co., Inc.
New York

editor
Paige Gilchrist

art director
Thom Gaines

consultant
Mary Weber

principal photography
Evan Bracken, Light Reflections

Richard Hasselberg,
Jolly Hasselberg Photography

editorial assistance
Veronika Alice Gunter
Roper Cleland

production assistance
Hannes Charen

Cover photo: Dana Schock and
Associates, Sudbury, MA; Dana
Schock, ASLA, architect/photographer

Library of Congress Cataloging-in-Publication Data

Gilchrist, Paige
    Making garden floors : stone, brick, tile, concrete, ornamental gravel,
recycled materials and more / Paige Gilchrist.
        p. cm.
    Includes index.
    ISBN 1-57990-212-x
        1. Patios—Design and construction—Amateurs' manuals. 2. Garden walks—
Design and construction—Amateurs' manuals. I. Title.

TH4970.G55 2001
690'.893--dc21

10 9 8 7 6 5 4 3 2 1

Published by Lark Books, a division of
Sterling Publishing Co., Inc.
387 Park Avenue South, New York, N.Y. 10016

© 2001, Lark Books

Distributed in Canada by Sterling Publishing,
c/o Canadian Manda Group, One Atlantic Ave., Suite 105
Toronto, Ontario, Canada M6K 3E7

Distributed in the U.K. by:
Guild of Master Craftsman Publications Ltd.
Castle Place
166 High Street
Lewes
East Sussex
England
BN7 1XU
Tel: (+ 44) 1273 477374
Fax: (+ 44) 1273 478606
Email: pubs@thegmcgroup.com
Web: www.gmcpublications.com

Distributed in Australia by Capricorn Link (Australia) Pty Ltd., P.O.
Box 6651, Baulkham Hills, Business Centre
NSW 2153, Australia

The written instructions, photographs, designs, patterns, and projects in this volume
are intended for the personal use of the reader and may be reproduced for that purpose only. Any other use, especially commercial use, is forbidden under law without
written permission of the copyright holder.

Every effort has been made to ensure that all the information in this book is accurate.
However, due to differing conditions, tools, and individual skills, the publisher cannot
be responsible for any injuries, losses, and other damages that may result from the use
of the information in this book.

If you have questions or comments about this book, please contact:
Lark Books
50 College St.
Asheville, NC 28801
(828) 253-0467

Manufactured in Hong Kong by Dai Nippon Printing, Ltd.

ISBN 1-57990-212-x

table of contents

introduction

There's no getting around it; gardens and yards are full of dirt. Which is to say, under certain weather conditions, they're full of mud. In any given landscape, they may also feature protruding rocks, exposed tree roots, half-hidden animal holes, and other hindrances to sure footing. All of which means that, if gardens and yards are also places where we want picnic tables and pools and grills, where we want to host parties and lounge around with good books and pad about comfortably in bare feet, we probably need to do a little something about all the dirt and other deterrents.

At its most basic, a garden floor is simply that little something—a level area meant to keep your feet clean and dry and your chair and your glass of iced tea upright. From a purely practical standpoint, a big plastic tarp or a few well-placed wooden planks would do it. If the idea is to keep grass clippings and clumps of earth from being tracked where they don't belong or to rig up a steady base for a seat, what more do you really need?

The truth, of course, is that few of us cultivate gardens or care for yards to satisfy only practical needs. We don't go out the back door to make do. We go out there to make homemade ice cream and grill corn on the cob, to serve visitors cold drinks, to eat dinner by candlelight, and to spend hours with the Sunday paper. When we walk outside into our gardens and yards, we continue entertaining and relaxing and playing and cooking and eating and living our lives. It makes sense, then, that the same impulse that drives us to rip up the orange shag carpet and put down hardwood inside would guide us when we move outdoors. We want our homes—indoors and out—to reflect who we are and how we like to live.

Garden floors, like their indoor counterparts, can define—or redefine—the entire character of a setting, whether you want

and lay an outdoor floor. How-to photographs, color illustrations, and step-by-step instructions take you from putting your first stake in the ground to building a solid foundation and settling your pavers firmly in place. Supporting chapters help you compare and contrast paving options and take you on a visual tour of the accessible list of tools you'll need for the job.

In eight detailed chapters that follow, we show you how to apply that technical information to create floors that not only function, but do so with flair—and in every form imaginable. We give you detailed specifics for installing basic floors of brick, tile, ornamental gravel and pebbles, various types of stone, concrete pavers, poured concrete, and recycled and nontraditional materials. But the basics are only the beginning. Each chapter also features dozens of full-color photographs that illustrate how the material and techniques have been adapted in a wide range of settings to create floors of all sizes, shapes, and styles.

to add elegance, incorporate whimsy, update a look that's outmoded, visually link scattered landscaping elements, or enliven a spot that's featureless. They take the form of everything from traditional brick terraces and rustic stone patios to mosaic-covered surfaces for potted plants and intimate seating areas paved with decorative pebbles. Think of them as outdoor rugs that provide the foundation for your garden room. Some are like elaborate tapestries. Others could be handwoven runners. Some serve as simple welcome mats. Still others are bold accent pieces. But all have the potential to perform the practical function of a floor and, at the same time, set the tone for your outdoor design.

Addressing those twin concerns of practicality and style is exactly what we had in mind when we put this book together. We start with a thorough overview of all the technical information you need to plan

Eventually, you'll want to put the book down and wander back to your own outdoor space. And yes, it may currently feature a boring concrete slab, a parched lawn—or just a tabula rasa of dirt. But chances are, after flipping through the pages that follow, it'll all look a bit different than it did before. Maybe, in addition to what's there, you're now also able to make out a picnic area of bluestone slabs under an arbor of wisteria vines. Or a patio of terra-cotta tile surrounding a fire pit. Or a quiet meditation garden paved with raked gravel. No telling what you'll see out there once you're armed with both inspiration and some simple techniques for bringing your vision to life.

planning your
design

If only there were an easy-to-follow formula for planning your garden floor's design. Maybe a nice, foolproof computer program that would allow you to key in a set of variables, hit "enter," and receive a perfectly tailored plan, complete with recommendations for your floor's location, shape, size, and paving material.

Then again, one of the main reasons we're lured away from the computer screen and all our other planning gadgets and out into the garden is that we like the more natural flow we find there. Rules are never quite as rigid as they seem inside. And that, oddly, makes everything a bit more clear. Once we've wandered around out there for awhile, it begins to dawn on us that we're not simply bringing together the right combination of pavers and mortar and decorative edging. We're creating a place where we'll drink lemonade with friends or serve birthday cake to five-year-olds or sit and quietly watch our garden grow—a place that will be likely be central to our living and our lives.

This going outside, in other words, and the subsequent wandering is essential to planning the design of your garden floor. It will, of course, lead to some actual pencil-to-paper plotting and figuring (we'll get to that at the end of this section). But for now, get out, walk around, and simply ponder three basic questions:

■ **How do you plan to use your garden floor?**

■ **What is your personal style?**

■ **What are the characteristics of your site?**

Following are some suggestions for exploring each question as you stroll.

your floor's use

■ What is the main purpose of your garden floor? If it's to serve as a base for a piece of garden sculpture, for example, your floor will likely be relatively small. If it's to provide a place for pool parties, on the other hand, you're embarking on a larger job.

■ Do you plan to use your floor frequently or only on special occasions? Your answer may influence the paving material you choose and what sort of foundation you create.

■ Do you plan to use your floor as an eating and entertaining area? If so, you may want it near the door that leads inside and toward the kitchen. You might also want to consider incorporating utilities such as electricity and running water as well as space for a grill into your plan.

TOP **Make sure your floor and its design are large enough to meet your needs.**

You'll have different design considerations, depending on whether you're creating a large parking terrace (MIDDLE), a secluded seating area (BOTTOM), or something in between.

your style

- What sort of look do you want in general? Classic and elegant? Contemporary? Charmingly lived-in? Consider the style of existing landscaping elements and of the architecture of your house as you answer these questions. Each paving material lends itself to a certain style. You'll also find that small details, such as growing moss in the joints between your pavers instead of mortaring them, can help set a specific tone.

- Are there other features you want to incorporate into your floor design, such as a hot tub or a fish pond?

- Do you want your floor to form the foundation for a quiet and meditative space? In this case, you may want it farther from the house.

- Will you place furniture on the floor? Think about what kind and how much; both will affect the size of your floor. Also, consider whether you want to incorporate seating into your design through seat walls or other structures.

- What time of day do you think you'll most often be using the floor? Pay attention to sun patterns and wind activity during that time of day; they may affect where you place your floor. If you'll be using your floor frequently in the evenings, you may want to incorporate lighting into your plan (which could involve installing wiring before you actually lay your floor).

LEFT Consider other features you want to incorporate into your design when you plan your floor.

■ On a more subtle level, what's the atmosphere you want to create? Shady and intimate (maybe even half hidden)? Sunny and open? One that beckons to early morning coffee drinkers? One that's hospitable to flocks of young swimmers and all of their pool paraphernalia?

■ Will you often entertain people wearing evening dress or parents pushing strollers? If so, you'll want to keep in mind that gravel and pebbles are hard on high heels and wheels. Pavers with unmortared joints can pose problems, too. A smooth surface will probably best suit your style.

■ How much interest do you have in caring for your floor? Would you prefer a floor that requires minimal mainte-nance (maybe sweeping off once a season), or is puttering (perhaps replen-ishing sand in the joints between bricks or raking gravel) a welcome bit of back-yard therapy for you?

■ How much money do you want to spend on your floor, and do you want to do all of the work yourself?

LEFT & ABOVE The same material, used differently in different settings, can look casu-ally rustic or formal and polished.

your site

- Study the structural elements on your site. In addition to your house, is there a deck, shed, wall, fence, or other structure your floor will share space with? Take into consideration their materials, sizes, colors, and textures, and think about how you want your floor to blend or contrast with these other elements.

- Study your site's natural and living features, from gardens and flower beds to trees and hedges. How do you want your floor to relate to them? Could it wrap around a favorite tree or connect to the path that winds through the rose garden? Is there a special view you'd like to be able to see from the patio?

- Walk your site after a good rain to see how well your soil drains. Check for especially soggy (poorly draining) areas, and notice your site's natural water runoff patterns. There's a lot you can do to improve drainage (see page 35), but you'll have the best success if you're working with rather than against your site's natural tendencies.

- Walk some more (you can do this when your site is dry), and get to know the topography of your site. Does it slope quite a bit? You might consider terraced floors with connecting steps. Is it completely flat? If so, you'll want to build in some slope to both aid drainage and add visual interest.

Do all of this walking at various times of day to get a sense of sun patterns, wind patterns, even noise patterns. What you find out may prompt you to consider incorporating screens, hedges, trellises, arbors, or even fences into your overall design. While you're at it, take a mental trip through the seasons that affect your site. Will there be times when your floor is subjected to heavy rains or lots of snow and ice—or will the sun beat down on it most of the year?

As you'll see in Chapter 2, page 18, some paving materials are better suited to harsh weather conditions, others drain better in wet climates.

Notice the circulation patterns throughout your site. Where do people naturally sit, stand, gather, and travel back and forth? They'll offer some of the most helpful clues of all about where to locate your floor and how to provide access to it.

The paving material you use—and how you use it—may depend on the atmosphere you want to create. The photos (ON THE FACING PAGE AND ABOVE) **show how decorative gravel alone can create a range of different moods.**

developing the plan

If your left brain is now demanding that you put something down on paper, you can go back inside, jot down what you observed, and prepare to make a scaled drawing.

Making a Scaled Drawing

A scaled drawing is simply a bird's-eye view of your site, on which a unit of measurement is equal to a longer dimension on the actual site. For example, one common formula is to let ⅛ inch (3 mm) on your plan represent 1 foot (30.5 cm) on the ground. If you have a survey of your house site, use it as your scaled drawing (increasing its size on a photocopy machine, if necessary). If not, create one for your site (or for only the portion where you think your floor will go, if you already have a clear idea).

1 Measure all existing structures and features (such as drives, walks, utilities, planting beds, and trees).

2 Use a pencil, ruler, and drafting triangle to transfer scaled versions of the structures and features to a piece of plain paper. (If your drawing is too big for a regular piece of paper, you can buy large vellum sheets for drawings of this sort at graphic supply stores. You can also use graph paper, which makes scaled drawings easy; let each square represent an actual dimension on the ground.)

ABOVE **Think about blending your garden floor with your site's natural and other landscaping elements.**

Adding Your Floor to the Drawing

A scaled base map allows you to play with options on paper, adjusting your floor's shape and size and moving it around (which is a whole lot easier than moving actual dirt and pavers).

1 Make several photocopies of your base map, or tape tracing paper over your master copy.

2 Armed with the information you gathered during all that time outside, begin sketching design ideas. Start with rough concepts, and refine them as you go—maybe a round patio becomes

an oval, or a seating area moves from one spot to a better one under a tree. Don't worry about the exact shape and size of your floor at this point.

3 Back outside! Take your plans out and evaluate them. Drag a chair with you, sit on the spot you've picked for your floor, and notice how it feels. Lay out a hose or stick survey flags in the ground to roughly mark the perimeter of the floor and see how it looks, both while you're standing in the space and when you view it from other points.

4 Once you're satisfied with your concept, pull out a clean copy of your base map (or tape a new sheet of tracing paper on top of your master), and draw your planned floor to scale in its exact position. Your final scaled drawing will help you calculate the amount of foundation and paving materials you need, and it will guide you as you lay your floor.

At this point, of course, your plan still has some blanks you need to fill in. The paving material you choose, the technique you use to lay it, and whether you add decorative touches such as edging or plants in the gaps between pavers will all affect your floor's design. The chapters that follow give you the details you need on materials and techniques. And the thinking you did earlier in this chapter provides a basis for sifting through those details, making decisions, and coming up with a complete plan for your project. But when you're outside once again, your shovel

finally in hand and a pile of paving materials nearby, don't be surprised to find yourself making minor adjustments and shifting your thinking now and then. Even the best drawn plans often become a little better once you're out there digging in the dirt. It's all part of that natural flow.

BELOW Let the topography of your site help guide your choices about material (poured concrete does well on this sloping terrain) and influence whether you incorporate terraced levels or other features into your design.

paving
materials

Nothing affects the character of your garden floor as much as the material you pave it with. Each choice creates a distinct look, from the old-world charm of recycled bricks and cobbles to the contemporary appeal of concrete. In addition, each material has its own pros and cons as far as ease of installation, cost, durability, and climate considerations. This chapter gives you an overview of the qualities of common paving materials, making it easy to compare, contrast, and determine which one is best for your project.

brick

The Look

With its plentiful range of colors and textures and diverse array of laying patterns, brick is one of the most versatile materials you can choose. Whether you want picturesque (maybe reclaimed brick from a former city street with plants creeping out of the joints), formal (try crisp new brick in a precise, traditional pattern), or something in between, chances are you can find a brick to achieve the effect.

Pros

Because of its standard size, brick is easier than randomly shaped stone to both quantify and lay. As a paving material, it provides a nice complement to brick houses and other structures, and it's often right at home in historic neighborhoods. Plus, it's easy to clean, and those with a rough texture create a surface with good traction. Brick also mixes well with other materials, from concrete to stone, and makes especially effective and attractive edging. Finally, if laid on a flexible foundation, a brick floor is relatively easy to remove if you find you must improve drainage or repair utilities beneath it.

Cons

Brick can be difficult to match if you want your new patio or terrace to blend perfectly with your home's exterior or an existing path or wall. Brick is also susceptible to efflorescence (white streaks), and light colors of brick can stain easily, because they're less dense and more absorbent. Frost heaves and growing tree roots can cause brick floors to buckle, and brick can crack under extreme weight.

Climate Considerations

Brick tends to grow mossy and slick in rainy climates, old bricks may crack or crumble in winter climates, and brick floors make for an especially hot surface for barefooted travelers in sunny climates.

Durability

If the quality of your brick is good, its durability will be good, too. Unfortunately, sometimes older brick with more character doesn't weather well. Bricks designed specifically for paving are the best choice. Paving bricks are pressed densely into molds by machine and baked longer than building bricks, making them less absorbent and, as a result, better for outdoor flooring.

Ease of Installation

To ensure a smooth brick surface, you need to invest the time in laying a firm foundation. And if you're laying your floor on a flexible (as opposed to a concrete) foundation, you can't do without edging, so you need to plan for that, too. Finally, laying brick requires careful attention to detail, especially if you're laying intricate patterns.

Calculating Quantity

Though they come in various sizes and thicknesses, brick pavers are typically $5/8$ to $2\frac{1}{4}$ inches (1.6 to 5.7 cm) thick, $3\frac{5}{8}$ inches (9.2 cm) wide, and $7\frac{5}{8}$ inches (19.4 cm) long. Using that standard size (and allowing for joints between the bricks), it takes approximately five bricks to pave a square foot (.3 square m) (this allows you a few extra for breakage or for replacing bricks in the future). Multiply the length of your floor by the width to

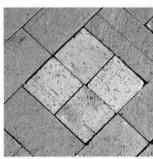

determine total square feet or meters (and remember that brick laid on edge, which creates a more unusual-looking surface, will cover less area).

Purchasing

You can get brick through brick suppliers, tile companies, and home-and-building supply centers. If you have a brick home or other brick you want to match, it's a good idea to take one brick home for comparison before you have an entire load delivered. Be sure you purchase paving bricks rather than facing bricks, which are intended for walls, and if you live in an area where temperatures dip below freezing, purchase SW (severe weather) bricks. With a full-sized pickup truck that's got good suspension, you can typically haul about 100 pounds (45 kg) or more of brick. Most suppliers also deliver for a fee, and many rent load-and-go vehicles that you can drive back to your site and unload.

Pricing

Because bricks are sold individually, the cost will depend on how many you need and what style you choose. The three most common colors—red, tan, and gray—sell for the same price, but the price of other styles and colors of brick will vary.

tile

The Look

Paving tiles range from natural, unglazed terra-cotta squares to less traditional shapes featuring brightly colored glazes and intricate patterns, all available in a multitude of sizes. Depending on the type you choose, you can use tiles to add regional flavor, ethnic flair, or whimsy, color, and fun to your garden setting.

Pros

Tiles made for exterior use, especially those that are unglazed, are very dense and highly resistant to scratching and marring. If you want to make glazed tiles

less slippery, you can add an abrasive coating. All except the lightest tiles resist dirt and staining. Best of all, tiles offer vivid colors and customized designs you can't find in other paving materials.

Cons

Because they're thin, tiles can't withstand much load, and without a well-prepared concrete foundation set with expansion joints (see page 47), they're susceptible to cracking. Tiles are also labor intensive to lay; you've got to grout between every joint, and custom-designed tiles, especially, can be expensive.

Climate Considerations

If your floor will have to withstand freezing and thawing, be sure you use tiles designed specifically for outdoor use. Also, the air and surface temperatures should be between 60 and 90 °F (16 and 32 °C) when you're installing tiles.

Durability

Without the most stable of foundations, tile is prone to cracking.

Ease of Installation

Creating a tile floor is more time-consuming than working with many paving materials. If you want your floor to last, you don't have the option of dry laying tile on a flexible foundation. You've got to first construct a concrete foundation, then mortar the tiles in place.

Calculating Quantity

Multiply the length of your floor by the width to determine the amount of tile you need in square feet or meters.

Purchasing

You'll find the best selection at centers that specialize in tile distribution. Some brick suppliers also sell tile. Again, be sure to specify vitreous or impervious tile for exterior use when you place your order. And choose tiles that have a non-skid surface.

Pricing

Tile is sold by the square foot or meter, with price depending on the material and design you choose. Clay tile such as terra-cotta, for example, is less expensive than quarried tile.

ornamental gravel & pebbles

The Look

This most eclectic category of paving material includes smooth water-washed pebbles dredged from riverbeds, bright white angular chippings from larger rocks, and much in between. You can find gravel or pebbles to blend—or contrast—with virtually any surrounding plants and landscaping elements. And any type you go with will create a garden floor with much more sense of movement than you get with a fixed paving material.

Pros

In addition to its versatility (at home everywhere from crisp, formal gardens to meditative rock gardens), loose rock is one of the least expensive materials you can choose. It also drains well, conforms easily to curving layouts and gentle slopes, holds its shape if the ground underneath it heaves, and acts as a mulch for surrounding plants.

Cons

If your stone is larger than ¾ inch (1.9 cm), it'll be difficult to walk on. In general, a floor of loose rock isn't the best choice for an area where you expect heavy traffic from strollers, wheelbarrows, or people sporting high-heeled shoes. Loose rock also tends to travel outside its borders, meaning periodic raking back in may be necessary—and edging is pretty much a must. If your garden floor is near the door and lots of tracking back and forth is common, it can even tend to migrate inside the house. Weeds can also pop up in a loose-rock floor, and pure white rocks can discolor over time.

Climate Considerations

Use the information beginning on page 35 to solve any drainage problems ahead of time if you're laying a loose-rock floor in a wet climate.

Durability

You'll need to replenish your rock occasionally and rake spillage back in place, but outside of this easy maintenance, loose-rock floors feature good durability.

Ease of Installation

Moderately easy—and much quicker than mortaring pavers in place. However, you should allow time, energy, and a budget for the step of installing edging around any gravel floor (it helps keep the rock from straying).

Calculating Quantity

Many types of loose rock are sold in bags by the cubic foot or meter. You can also purchase bulk amounts in cubic yards or tons. To figure the amount of rock you need in cubic feet or meters, multiply the width and length of your floor layout by how deep you want your rock, keeping all measurements in feet or meters. Divide cubic feet by 27 to convert to cubic yards.

Purchasing

Sand and gravel yards and quarries sell a variety of loose rock in bulk; you can cart it home in a truck or have it delivered for a fee. You can also often find smaller amounts of loose rock (usually sold by the bag) at nurseries and home-and-garden centers.

Pricing

You'll get the best prices by buying in bulk—typically by the ton (2000 lbs or 907 kg). Special, decorative stone will cost you more than standard gravel.

stone

Natural stone pavers come in three major categories: fieldstone, flagstone, and cut stone. Fieldstone is just what the name suggests—rough, irregular, uncut stone collected from fields, streambeds, or old stone walls. For paving projects, you want smooth, flat fieldstones. Flagstone is quarried stone that is flat, thin, and cut or broken into irregular shapes, typically with jagged, angular edges. Cut stone (also called ashlar), is cut into uniform shapes, usually squares or rectangles ranging in size from about 1 square foot to 4 square feet (.3 square m to 1.2 square m).

There are four main types of stone; availability of each type varies by region.

SEDIMENTARY STONES, such as sandstone, limestone, and bluestone, are somewhat soft and easy to cut. They can feature intricate patterns and a textured surface that's non-slippery. However, they are subject to staining and weathering because they are so porous.

SLATE is a hard and durable stone, ranging in color from blue to gray to black. It's thinly cut, so it's best laid only on a concrete foundation.

GRANITE is very hard and durable. Colors range from white to pink to dark gray. It's an expensive material, but useful for edging and surfacing.

MARBLE is an expensive stone with stunning colors and patterns. It's easy to cut, but can make for a slippery paved surface.

The Look

Fieldstone is the material to use if you're after a rustic, heavily textured floor that looks as if it was lifted from the yard of a quaint country cottage and placed among the flowers in your garden. Flagstone, with its random shapes and aged surfaces, creates a similar effect, but gives you a more even surface. Both lend themselves to imaginative patterns, with lots of irregular gaps in between the stones—perfect for plantings if you're laying your floor on a flexible (rather than concrete) foundation. Cut stone, on the other hand, with its uniform shape and size, will typically create a more elegant and formal-looking floor. In all cases, if you use a type of stone found in your area, your floor will more naturally blend with its surroundings.

Pros

You can use fieldstone and flagstone on both level and gently sloping surfaces. Flagstone is easy to cut and shape as you piece together the puzzle of your floor (see page 93). Cut stone creates a very smooth surface (ideal if your floor will be home to lots of outdoor furniture). And if it's mortared in place, it becomes a nearly permanent surface. Choosing any of these stone types gives you an opportunity to build your floor with locally available material and to blend your floor with other stone elements in your landscape.

Cons

Stones (particularly fieldstones) that have irregular surfaces will collect puddles when it rains, and they can be difficult to walk on if they're extremely bumpy. Very smooth pavers, on the other hand, such as slate and marble, become slick when they're wet. Cut stone can also be expensive. Oh, and stone is typically heavy.

Climate Considerations

In winter climates, the puddles that collect on the surfaces of uneven stones will form pools of ice, creating walking hazards; small, dry-laid stones will be subject to frost heaves; and cut stone can crack.

Durability

Good to excellent, though some types of stone (limestone, for example) will wear down under years of weathering and use.

Ease of Installation

Laying fieldstone or flagstone is a bit like putting together a very large—and very heavy—jigsaw puzzle. Because each piece is different, you may find yourself spending a lot of time cutting and shaping your stones so they fit the way you want them to. Cut stone will be slightly easier to dry lay, but mortaring it in place is a labor-intensive (and again, heavy) undertaking.

Calculating Quantity

Multiply the length of your floor by its width to determine the amount of stone you need in square feet or meters. Fieldstone and flagstone are usually sold by the ton, but your figure in square feet or meters will give your supplier enough information to roughly calculate the amount you need.

Purchasing

If you're lucky enough to have a stone-studded field, you can collect fieldstones yourself (though it could be a time-consuming job, depending on the size of your floor). Stone yards are also a good source for all types of paving stone, and some tile companies sell cut stone, as well. Suppliers will typically load your truck or car with small amounts of stone. Many also offer delivery for a fee.

Pricing

If the stone you're buying is sold by the ton, size and thickness of the stone will affect the price. Some colors and types are also more expensive than others, with rare colors of cut stone being the most expensive of all. Also, you'll pay a premium if you want to hand-pick your stones at a stone yard.

concrete pavers

The Look

Concrete pavers have become wildly popular because they lend themselves to nearly any look. Some are excellent imitations of natural stone, with the real thing's range of colors and textures. Others come in artificial shapes, from circles to hexagons, or feature faux stamped finishes that mimic materials such as brick or wood. You can also find concrete pavers in block form resembling brick or granite. Finally, specially designed interlocking concrete pavers have an artificial but neat (and exceptionally sturdy) design.

Pros

Lay your pavers properly on a well-prepared foundation, and your floor can last for decades with very little maintenance. Concrete pavers can withstand severe weather and heavy loads without losing their color or structural integrity. What's more, they're about half the cost of stone pavers. They're also easier to cut than brick if you need to shape them to fit your floor space, and they lend themselves to intricate and interesting laying patterns. If you're laying your pavers on a flexible foundation, it will be relatively easy to remove a section temporarily, if necessary, to improve drainage or reach any utility lines running below the floor.

Cons

Poor-quality pavers trying to imitate brick or some other material can create an unnatural look, and wide expanses of interlocking concrete pavers may have a monotonous effect. Also, with pavers you should plan for the extra step of installing edging to help hold them in place.

Climate Considerations

Prepare your foundation properly, and concrete pavers will work well in any climate.

Durability

Excellent.

Ease of Installation

Because of their uniform size and shape, concrete pavers are somewhat easier to lay than fieldstone or flagstone, but mortaring them in place, if you choose to do so, is still a labor-intensive undertaking. Laying non-interlocking concrete blocks is quite similar to the detailed work of laying brick; interlocking concrete pavers are much easier to lay. And again, investing the time and work preparing a good foundation to start with is key.

Calculating Quantity

Pavers are sold by the square foot or meter. Multiply the length of your floor by its width to determine the amount you need. Paving blocks are slightly smaller than standard-size bricks, but you can still calculate quantity the same way you would for brick, figuring on approximately five blocks to pave a square foot (.3 square m).

Purchasing

Concrete material suppliers are your best bet for purchasing pavers. Pavers are also often sold at home-and-building supply centers. Some distribution centers have demonstration areas, where laid sections of pavers make it easy to evaluate different colors and styles.

Pricing

You'll spend about the same amount on concrete pavers as you would on brick, and considerably less than you would on stone.

poured concrete

The Look

Sometimes referred to as "liquid stone," the cement-and-water mixture that hardens into concrete can be poured into any form imaginable. It can also be colored, texturized with everything from floats and brooms to imprints of leaves, stamped with patterns, and embedded with materials from random shells to elaborate tile mosaics. Though it lends itself easily to urban and contemporary settings, it can be adapted to many others.

Pros

In addition to being one of the most cost-effective paving materials, concrete makes for a highly durable and long-lasting garden

floor that requires very little maintenance. Its design versatility is a big plus; it also combines well with other materials to create interesting patterns and unique finishes.

Cons

It's true. Concrete can look sterile if it's used unimaginatively in large, sweeping sections. It's also a more complicated paving material to work with than others; beginners may want some help (a well-prepared foundation is crucial). And, once concrete is in, it's in. If you change your mind about what you've done, you'll need to break up your floor and start over.

Climate Considerations

Cracking concrete can be a problem in harsh winter climates (or on sites with growing tree roots). Concrete can also ice over in the winter. You may want to watch the weather as you plan for pouring your floor, as well. Extremes of heat and cold can cause damage during the concrete's "curing."

Durability

Excellent.

Ease of Installation

Concrete floors are more time-consuming to create than any other. They also require more careful planning and more equipment.

Calculating Quantity

You can use either premixed cement, which comes in bags (you simply add water), or bulk materials (Portland cement, sand, and aggregate) that you mix yourself in a rented mixer (or a wheelbarrow for small amounts). A bag of premix will typically tell you how much coverage it provides. If you're buying in bulk, your supplier can help you figure out how much you need, which may vary, depending on what region you live in. Start with the standard formula: multiply the length by the width and depth of your floor and foundation area to determine the cubic feet or meters you need to cover (dividing by 27 if you want to convert cubic feet to cubic yards). With cement, add 10 percent to your total for spillage or waste.

Purchasing

Home-and-building supply centers sell bagged cement. If you're buying bulk materials and mixing them yourself, you can get the cement from a building supply store or a concrete materials supplier, and the sand and aggregate from a sand-and-gravel yard, all sold in cubic yards or by the ton. For larger jobs, it may be worthwhile to have a concrete supplier mix and deliver your cement.

Pricing

Overall, concrete is one of the least expensive paving materials. Use pre-mixed bags only for small jobs (they're too pricey for big ones). For other jobs, it may be a bit more expensive but worth the time savings to have a supplier deliver ready-mix cement. The cost will depend on your location, ease of access to your site, and the size of your order.

paving
tools

I f a quick word-association exercise has you linking the *floor* in garden floors with words such as *house* or *building* and then, worriedly, *construction site*, *work crews*, and *large, expensive equipment,* this is the chapter to read to set your mind at ease.

The list of tools you need to lay a basic garden floor is surprisingly short—not to mention familiar. If you've already tackled a do-it-yourself project involving measuring and marking and some digging and moving of dirt, chances are you've got most of what you need. None of the tools required is specialized or hard to find. In fact, most are so common you could buy those you don't already have at bargain prices at a good flea market—or borrow them from a friendly neighbor.

Following is an overview of all you'll need for each of the major stages of building a floor. In addition, at the beginning of each chapter on specific kinds of floors (starting on page 52), we let you know about additional tools you might need for that type of project. Some of those are one-time-use pieces of equipment (such as brick saws or power compactors) that you won't want to buy; you can easily rent those items at a local equipment rental service.

marking tools

PIN FLAGS (also called survey flags) or **STAKES AND STRING**. Use these markers to outline the perimeter of your planned floor. Simply stick the flags in the ground at regular intervals, or pound in wooden stakes or lengths of rebar at the corners and run a taut string from marker to marker. For a floor with a rounded or curving shape, you may want to use a rope or a garden hose as the marker, instead.

LEFT TO RIGHT: **marking paint, level, line levels, tape measure, carpenter's square, smaller level, pin flags, rebar and string**

TAPE MEASURE. To know exactly where to plant your flags or stakes (and for numerous other measuring jobs throughout the floor-building process), you'll need a good, sturdy measuring tool. A standard-model tape measure with a 25-foot (7.5 m) retractable steel tape is ideal.

CARPENTER'S SQUARE OR FRAMING SQUARE. These tools, which feature right angles, will help you quickly test the squareness of any corners in your floor's layout.

MARKING PAINT. Once you've marked the perimeter of your floor with flags, stakes, or a hose, you'll want to spray the lines on the ground, so you've got a guide when you start digging. (You could also snap a chalk line if you're marking a straight line between two points.)

FOUR-FOOT (1.2 M) LEVEL. You'll use this must-have tool to check the slope of your floor at every stage of the process, beginning with the grading of the site you're marking. If you already own a slightly smaller or larger level, what you have should work fine.

LINE LEVEL (ALSO CALLED A STRING LEVEL). This small, lightweight device that clips onto a taut string does the same job as a 4-foot (1.2 m) level, but it's handier for leveling longer stretches of your floor.

LEFT TO RIGHT: **square-bladed shovel, hand tamper, mattock, round-nose shovel**

excavating tools

ROUND-NOSE SHOVEL. For good, old-fashioned digging, you can't beat this all-purpose tool. You'll also reach for it when you're spreading foundation materials into the excavated area later.

SQUARE-BLADED SHOVEL. This shovel is good for cutting out the edges of your floor and leveling rough spots—and later for scooping crushed rock to fill your foundation.

MATTOCK. A broad, slightly curved digging blade at one end and a small chopping blade or pick at the other make a mattock the perfect tool for loosening packed earth and embedded rocks and cutting out roots.

HAND TAMPER. You'll need to compact your floor's foundation to start with, then tamp down each layer of the foundation materials as you add them to create a firm base for your paving material. Hand tampers feature metal plates that are typically 8 or 10 inches (20.3 or 25.4 cm) square. For an especially large site, you may want to rent a power compactor.

WHEELBARROW. You'll need a wheelbarrow for hauling out dirt at this stage and for hauling in materials to fill the foundation at the next one. If you'll be mixing concrete, get a heavy-duty wheelbarrow.

Other optional excavating tools include lopping shears or a pruning saw, which are helpful in cutting back small roots, and a foot adze hoe, useful for skimming the sod off the surface of your site and for breaking up clay.

LEFT TO RIGHT: **metal rake, mason's chisel, rubber mallet**

foundation material & paving tools

METAL RAKE. We're not talking about a leaf rake here; you need one you can put some force behind. As you begin dumping in loads of crushed rock and later sand to fill the floor's foundation, you'll use the teeth of this versatile tool to spread the material into place and the other side to smooth and level it.

SCREED. Forget the fancy name. A screed is simply a scrap piece of 2 x 4 you'll drag across your foundation's sand setting bed or across just-poured concrete to level the surface. When you're leveling a setting bed, you'll want to cut notches out of each end of your screed, so it fits over your floor's edging (or temporary supports such as metal pipes) and levels the sand to the appropriate height.

RUBBER MALLET. After laying your pavers, this is just the hand tool you need to tap them and settle them in.

MASON'S CHISEL. When working with some pavers, especially flagstone, you can use a mason's chisel to carefully chip them here and there (or score them and make clean cuts), helping them to better fit in place.

CLOCKWISE FROM LEFT: **stiff-bristled broom, brush, trowels**

finishing tools

STIFF-BRISTLED BROOM. A broom is indispensable for sweeping sand into your floor's joints (a small stiff-bristled brush can help in tight areas, too)—and for cleaning the surface of your floor when you're finished.

TROWELS. With their variety of shapes and sizes, trowels come in handy for everything from spreading out mortar beds for laying paving materials to neatly filling the joints in between them.

HOSE. A fine spray of water will help settle floors of pavers laid with sand or dry mortar in the joints.

Ear, eye, and knee protection

safety tools

Eye protection is important if you're chipping bricks or cutting stones. Add ear protection if you're using power equipment for either job or if you're operating a power compactor. Knee pads make kneeling in sand for hours as you carefully position pavers a much more comfortable undertaking. And sturdy work gloves make everything from carrying rocks to swinging a mattock happier tasks.

floor
basics

Just like the ones that keep us upright and comfortable inside, outdoor floors, whatever the type, need to be level and dry. That means well before you begin busying yourself with paving materials, you've got to devote some attention to slope, drainage, and preparing a proper foundation.

slope

Too Much

Every garden floor needs to slope somewhat (we'll get to that in a minute). But slope is also one of those good things you *can* have too much of.

If the patch of ground where you want to put your patio slants just slightly more than is comfortable for walking, standing, or sitting, you can smooth the grade fairly simply. Use a mattock to loosen the earth, a square-bladed shovel to skim soil from high spots, and a wheelbarrow to carry it to places you need to build up to make the site more level.

If, on the other hand, the place you've picked for your patio features a steep, downhill drop, an uphill climb, or lots of undulating contours, you may want to either rent a small, front-end-loading garden tractor to even it out or hire a professional grader. (These are also options if your site is just plain too big to tackle with a shovel.) When faced with a whole lot more slope than you want, however, remember that working *with* what you've got (rather than fighting it) will produce the least expensive and most natural-looking results. Instead of using heavy machinery to completely rearrange the grade on a large chunk of your yard, for example, you might want to consider putting in terraced garden floors linked by steps. The box on page 34 tells you how to build some simple steps to connect one floor to another along a steeply sloped area. If your job is a more complicated one, you'll probably want input and perhaps hands-on help from a landscape architect or a contractor.

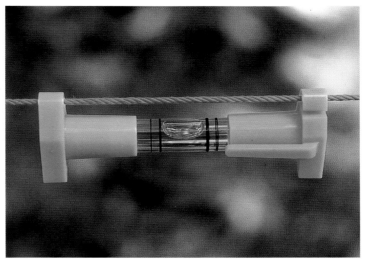

A string level with the air bubble resting in the center (indicating a level line)

Just Enough

Though you do need to even out steep slopes when you're laying a garden floor, a *completely* flat piece of ground is not what you're after. A gently sloping site is critical for directing water off the surface of your floor (and away from a nearby house or building foundation). A standard two-percent slope is nearly imperceptible to the eye (not to mention the feet), but it's just enough to direct water flow. To achieve it, grade your site, adding soil or skimming it away as necessary, so it falls about ¼ inch per foot of horizontal distance (1 cm per 30 cm).

To establish a two-percent slope for your site, use a string level with double lines attached to the middle of a taut string tied to two stakes, one at what should be the high end of your floor site (near your house foundation, for example), the other at the low end:

■ First, level the line, so the air bubble in the level rests in the center of the vial (photo 1).

■ Next, adjust the line (see figure 1) so the bubble in the vial rests against the outer line on the level's vial, reflecting a two-percent slope (or a ¼-inch [6 mm] drop per horizontal foot [30.5 cm]). If, for example, you're planning a patio that will be 12 feet (3.6 m) wide, the top edge of the site needs to be 3 inches (7.6 cm) higher than the bottom edge.

FIGURE 1 **Adjusting a string level to establish a two-percent slope**

adding simple steps

Often, rises and dips in a garden land-scape add visual interest you want to pre-serve. Rather than flattening your space into a featureless slab, you can level areas where you want to put paving, then connect them to others with informal steps cut into natural slopes. Spaced-landing timber steps are some of the simplest.

1 Clear the step area of plants, leaves, and topsoil.

2 Measure the distance in height be-tween the spots where you want the top and bottom steps.

3 Divide the measurement by the step height (the width of your timbers) to get the number of steps you need.

4 Install the timbers, spacing them evenly and working from the bottom of the slope to the top, compacting the soil behind each timber as you go.

5 Before anchoring the timbers, walk the steps to make sure the layout is comfortable. Once you're satisfied, drill two ⅝-inch (1.6 cm) holes through the center of each timber about 6 inches (15.2 cm) in from each end. Drive 24-inch (61 cm) pieces of #5 rebar down through the holes into the ground below until they're flush with the top of the timber.

Flat pieces of fieldstone installed by exca-vating spots for them to fit into the slope also make stable and especially natural-looking steps.

When you excavate your site to lay your floor's foundation, use the sloped string as a guide (measuring from the string down to the base of the foundation), to make sure the foundation floor is sloping appropriately.

You can also use a 4-foot-long (1.2 m) level with double lines on the vial to monitor the slope of the foundation as you excavate and, later, to monitor the slope of your paving material as you lay it:

■ Place the level so that one end sits at the high end of your site.

■ When the ground is sloping two percent, the level's air bubble will rest against the outer line on the level's vial (see figure 2). As you grade (working your way down the site's slope), periodically rest the level on the ground and adjust the soil, as necessary, to achieve your two-percent slope.

drainage

In addition to sloping your site so that rainwater will flow gently off your future floor's surface, you'll also want to check for any serious drainage problems, and, if necessary, improve your site's drainage before you lay your floor. If your site is plagued by large amounts of storm water runoff or subsurface water, you probably have one or more telltale signs, such as muddy areas, persistent puddles, particularly lush growth, or wet basement walls.

FIGURE 2 **Using a level to check slope**

You can also conduct this simple test to determine how well your site's soil drains.

1 Dig a hole roughly 4 inches (10.2 cm) in diameter by 2 feet (61 cm) deep, and fill it with water.

2 Let the water drain, then fill the hole with water again.

3 After 24 hours, check the hole. If all the water is gone, the soil is porous or sandy and drains well. If there is still standing water after 48 hours, the soil is too dense or full of clay; you'll want to improve its drainage before laying your floor. If the water in the hole gradually rises instead of falls, the site's water table is very high, making it a less than ideal spot for laying a floor directly in the ground; a floor constructed on a raised wooden platform might be a good alternative.

Improving drainage is always a site-specific job, but in general, identifying the nature of your drainage problem will help you determine the best way to correct it. Here are some basic solutions to common drainage problems.

Splash Blocks and Downspout Extensions

Make sure your roof downspouts are effectively directing water away from your house and not dumping it into the soil right at the foundation. If they're not directing water away, you can often correct the problem by placing purchased concrete splash blocks or several large stones at the places where the spouts release water; the splashblocks or stones will help dissipate the water. On a properly sloped site, you may also be able to solve the problem by simply adding a 2 to 4-foot (.6 to 1.2 m) downspout extension.

Drainpipes

You can lay a flexible, non-perforated, PVC drainpipe underground to solve a surface-water problem that doesn't respond to splashblocks or downspout extensions. Dig a 12-inch-deep (30.5 cm) trench running

FIGURE 3 **You can lay a drainpipe to solve a surface-water problem.**

from the source of the problem to an appropriate place for runoff water to drain. (You can use a special adaptor to connect the drainpipe to a downspout outlet, if necessary.) Storm sewers, community gutters, and the dry wells and catch basins described later in this section are good spots for directing the water. Sanitary sewers aren't, and directing runoff water onto a neighbor's property is not only impolite, but in many areas it's illegal. Make the trench 4 inches (10.2 cm) wider than the drainpipe, and slope it a minimum of $\frac{1}{8}$ inch (3 mm) per horizontal foot (30.5 cm). Lay 2 inches (5.1 cm) of gravel in the trench, install the pipe, cover it with more gravel, then add grass or plantings on top.

You can also use drainpipes to redirect subsurface water. Prepare a trench like the one described above, but lay a perforated PVC drainpipe, with the holes in the pipe facing down, so water will rise into the pipe and the holes won't become clogged with silt and debris.

Swales

Digging a shallow trench known as a swale is a good way to slow or redirect runoff water that courses down a hillside. Pitch it in the direction you want the water to go, mound and compact the soil on the downhill side, then re-lay your sod or plant over the trench with ground cover. To control erosion in a particularly steep swale, line it with landscape cloth that's specifically designed for erosion control and/or with rock (4 to 8-inch [10.2 to 20.3 cm] river rock or fieldstone works well).

FIGURE 4 **A swale is a good way to slow or redirect runoff water.**

Catch Basins

To improve the drainage of a low spot where constant puddling is a problem, a catch basin is your best bet. Catch basins are typically about 1 or 2 feet (.3 to .6 m) square and 2 to 6 feet (.6 to 1.2 m) deep. You can either pour your own concrete basin or purchase a plastic one. Install a sloping drainpipe to carry water from the catch basin to a drainage spot and put a grate on top, so you can clean silt and debris out of the basin periodically.

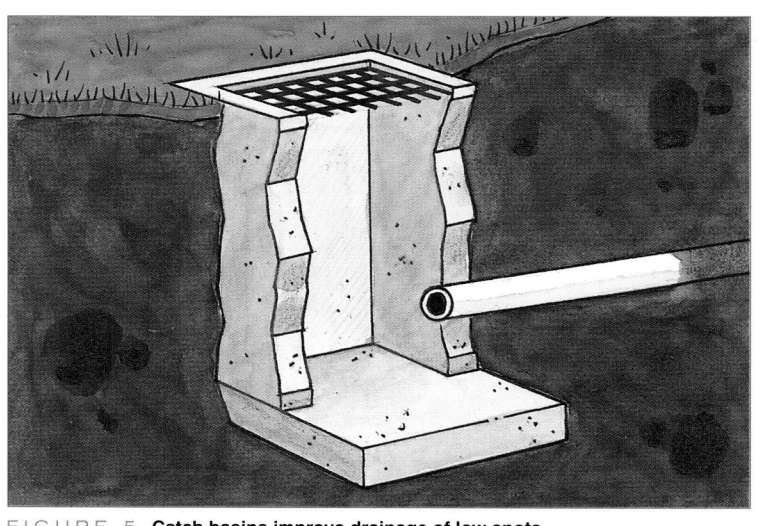

FIGURE 5 **Catch basins improve drainage of low spots.**

Dry Wells

If you don't have a good location for emptying water you've diverted with a drain or a swale, you can dig a dry well. It's a gravel-filled hole approximately 3 feet (.9 m) deep and 2 to 4 feet (.6 to 1.8 m) wide that is covered with landscape fabric, then topped with a layer of gravel or topsoil and sod. (See figure 6, page 38.)

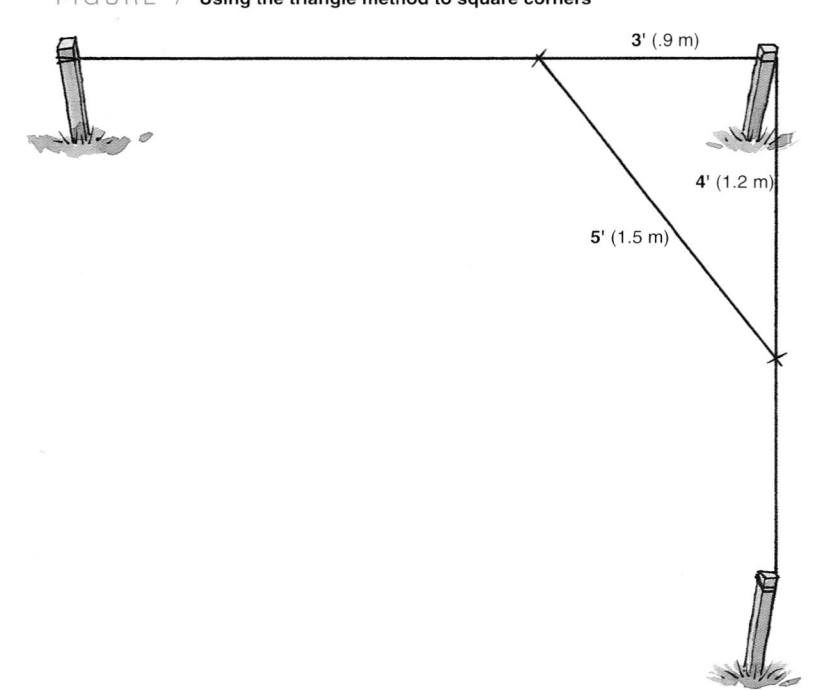

FIGURE 6 **Dig a dry well for emptying diverted water.**

FIGURE 7 **Using the triangle method to square corners**

3' (.9 m)

4' (1.2 m)

5' (1.5 m)

marking the design

Once you've assessed your site's slope and solved any drainage problems, you're ready to mark out your floor. If leveling your site requires some major grading, you may want to smooth and clear the ground and even out the slope of the overall area before this step. If not, you can mark your site first, then simply slope the floor's foundation as you excavate it.

For informal shapes featuring curves, use rope or a garden hose to mark your floor's outline. If your floor features straight edges, use a tape measure to plot its exact position, then mark the perimeter with stakes and string or with pin flags (also called survey flags). (Be sure to mark the perimeter several inches or centimeters outside your planned floor if you're pouring a concrete floor, which requires that you put form boards around the edges.) To square up the corners, apply a bit of basic geometry known as the triangle method: measure 3 feet (.9 m) along one leg of the triangle formed by the corner and mark that point; measure 4 feet (1.2 m) along the other leg of the triangle and mark that point; the diagonal between the two points will measure 5 feet (1.5 m) if the corner is square (see figure 7).

PHOTO 2 **Marking the floor outline with paint**

If you need to mark a precise, circular shape, use a stake and string as a compass, and place stakes at 1-foot (.3 m) intervals along the resulting arc.

After outlining your floor, use the rope, hose, or string lines as guides and mark the ground with powdered chalk, lime, sand, or marking paint. The marked lines will be easy to follow as you begin to dig out your floor's foundation (photo 2).

preparing the foundation

A strong, well-constructed foundation helps keep your garden floor stable and firm, it minimizes cracking and settling of your paving material, and it aids the area in draining properly. In short, you can't do without it. Whether you're creating a flagstone patio, a brick pad to put your picnic table on, or any other type of floor, you'll start the same way: by excavating your marked-out area and then adding materials to prepare one of three foundation options.

making a move

As you clear, smooth, and grade the site that will become your garden floor, chances are, you'll come up against existing plants and perhaps even a tree or two. It's best for them, easiest for you, and often much more interesting in terms of overall design if you simply leave them where they are and incorporate them into your plan. Wrap a patio around a towering oak, for example, and your new floor has good shade and an instant focal point. Try not to cut or fill more than a couple of inches or centimeters around the base of the tree, since most of the roots grow just under the surface. (The roots generally extend to the drip line of the tree, which is the area beneath the entire canopy.)

When you do have to move a plant or a tree to make room for your floor, prepare a spot for replanting it ahead of time, or ready a temporary place, then replant it permanently later. Spring and fall are the best times of year for relocating trees and shrubs; cloudy days and late afternoons or evenings offer the most ideal conditions. To remove a plant, shrub, or small tree, use a sharp spade to cut a circle around the roots, then shape the roots and their surrounding soil into a ball by undercutting the lower roots. Pick up the tree or shrub by the base of the root ball, not by the trunk; the weight of the soil can damage the roots. Put the transplant into the hole you prepared in its new location, and water it well. If you've got a large tree to relocate, enlist the help of a professional.

PHOTO 3 **Making vertical cuts with a square-bladed shovel**

excavating the foundation

If you've ever moved soil with a shovel, you've got all the specialized training you need to take on this step. The goal is to hollow out a base that is deep enough to hold your foundation materials and your paving material. The depth will vary from floor to floor, depending on the type and amount of foundation materials you're using (standard "recipes" follow), the thickness of your paving material, and the amount you want your floor surface to rise above the surrounding grade (½ to 1 inch [1.3 to 2.5 cm] is standard; however, if you're laying a floor that abuts the door to a house, you want the floor's surface to be 1 inch [2.5 cm] below the door sill). For a typical project, you'll excavate a foundation 6 to 10 inches (15.2 to 25.4 cm) deep.

You can start with a sod cutter to remove the top layer of your ground's organic matter if you have a lawn, or you can simply make vertical cuts with a square-bladed shovel. Once you're down to packed earth, try a mattock or foot adze hoe to loosen the soil, remove rocks embedded in the ground, and cut out small roots (photos 3 and 4). Toss what you excavate into a wheelbarrow as you go, and move it to a nearby storage spot. It'll come in handy later for backfilling your floor's edging and for adjusting the slope of the foundation floor, if necessary. At this stage, you should also excavate a

PHOTO 4 **Loosening the soil with a mattock**

PHOTO 5 **Excavating a trench around the foundation for edging**

PHOTO 6 **Checking the slope of the foundation**

PHOTO 7 **Tamping the soil**

trench around the perimeter of your floor for setting edging, if you plan to use it (photo 5) (see Adding Edging, page 46). Measure the depth of your edging material, then subtract the amount you want it to sit above the ground surface to determine how deep to dig the edging trench.

Once you reach the point of smoothing out and leveling your foundation floor, be sure to use a level to check its slope (photo 6), and adjust it as necessary to achieve the standard two-percent fall described on page 33. Finish by tamping and firming the soil well (photo 7). A poorly compacted foundation can cause settling and unevenness in a floor's surface. For a large area, you may want to rent a power compactor, but for most home projects, a hand tamper works fine. You can also do a lot of good tamping with nothing more than a couple of feet. (It's best if you wear work boots rather than tennis shoes for the job.)

PHOTO 8 **Adding the foundation's first layer: crushed rock**

adding foundation materials

Option 1: Flexible Foundation of Rock and Sand

A flexible foundation of rock and sand is the most common type used for home yard and garden projects. It's durable, yet flexible enough to withstand most frost heaves, and it provides a stable underpinning for either dry laying or mortaring in place any paving material.

Begin with a layer of crushed rock or gravel. Use an even mix of washed rock pieces ranging from a maximum of ¾ inch (1.9 cm) to fine particles. In most cases, a 2 to 4-inch (5.1 to 10.2 cm) layer of crushed rock is sufficient. If your soil drains poorly, make the crushed-rock layer of the foundation about 2 inches (5.1 cm) deeper, and if you're laying a drive or some other surface that will need to accommodate vehicles, make this bottom layer of rock 6 to 10 inches (15.2 to 25.4 cm) deep. For an extra-strong foundation, instead of crushed rock you can substitute the same material your local grading contractors use for road bases, called road bond or ABC (aggregate base course). Be sure to specify that

PHOTO 9 **Spreading and leveling the crushed rock**

PHOTO 10 **Checking the depth of the foundation's first layer**

you want the road base mix used in the top rather than the bottom of the road base. And use this mixture only if you have well-draining soil; because it compacts so densely, it doesn't provide much percolation. Spread and level this first layer of base material with a shovel and rake, checking to make sure you're maintaining a two-percent slope (photos 8 through 10).

If you're especially concerned about weed growth, spread non-woven landscape fabric over the layer of crushed stone and into your edging trenches. The fabric will also help keep the sand, added next, from settling into the stone layer. Overlap sheets of the landscape fabric, as necessary, and cut 1-inch (2.5 cm) holes in it every 12 inches (30.5 cm), so the foundation will drain well.

Set your edging material in place (photo 11). (See Adding Edging, page 46.)

PHOTO 11 **Setting edging and checking to make sure it's level**

calculating quantity for foundation material

You can buy the crushed rock and sand you need to build your floor foundation at a sand and gravel yard. Suppliers typically sell by the cubic yard, cubic foot (or cubic meter), or the ton, and they'll be glad to help you calculate the amount you need. If you want to come up with an estimate yourself, here's the formula to follow.

1 Multiply the length of your floor by its width to determine your floor's surface area. (If your floor is circular, multiply its radius squared by 3.14 to determine the area.)

2 Multiply the surface area of your floor by the depth of crushed rock or sand you need, converting the depth from inches or centimeters to feet or meters before multiplying. The result is the amount of material you need in cubic feet (or cubic meters).

For example, say you have a patio that is 12 feet by 12 feet in surface area and you want to add 3 inches of crushed rock. You would multiply 12 by 12 by .25 to come up with 36 cubic feet. (You divide the depth in inches by 12 to convert it to feet before multiplying.)

3 If you'd like to convert the results of step 2 to cubic yards, simply divide the number of cubic feet by 27. (For example, 36 divided by 27 is 1.33 cubic yards.)

Once you've got your figure, increase it. You should always order approximately 10 percent more loose base material than the compacted volume you want to end up with, to allow for the compaction and any settling.

PHOTO 12 **Adding the sand setting bed on top of the crushed rock**

PHOTO 13 **Smoothing and leveling the sand setting bed with a rake**

PHOTO 14 **Checking the setting bed's level**

Spread on 1 inch (2.5 cm) of clean, washed, coarse concrete sand. This final layer is the setting bed for your paving material. If you have a source of river sand, it will also work well for this layer, but don't use fine mason's sand or the silica sand sold by the bag at home improvement stores. Save finer sand for filling the joints between your paving material later. Rock dust, also known as granite fines and available from quarries in certain regions, makes a good setting bed, as well. Don't rely on this final layer as a leveling layer; rather, make sure your foundation is level and properly sloped before adding the sand (photo 12).

Smooth the sand setting bed with a rake. You can also spray it with water to gently compact it. Then level it (photos 13 and 14). If you're planning to lay thick, heavy paving stone, you can level the sand by simply dragging the flat end of your rake over the surface. If, instead, you're preparing the bed for brick, tile, or another surface material that requires a more precise and uniform level, drag a screed across the surface (see figure 8). For areas that are too large to rest the notched ends of the screed on the edging material as you move it across the sand, set up temporary boards or even long, thin, metal pipes, and move them as you screed the entire surface.

Figure 9 shows a side view of a flexible foundation of rock and sand.

Option 2: Flexible Foundation of Sand Only

For smaller jobs on sites that feature good drainage and a solid subgrade, you can adapt the full flexible foundation recipe above, and lay a foundation of sand only (eliminating the crushed rock). This scaled-down version is easier and less expensive to lay, but it's also less stable. It's best for areas that won't be getting a lot of pedestrian traffic—maybe a small floor where you'll stand a birdbath, for example. Don't ever lay a sand-only foundation for a floor that will have to accommodate vehicle traffic.

If you choose to use it, spread the non-woven landscape fabric directly on the foundation soil.

Spread on 2 inches (5.1 cm) of sand or rock dust.

Set your edging material in place, if you're using edging.

FIGURE 8 **Using a screed to achieve a precise level on the setting bed.**

Smooth the sand setting bed with a rake, spray it with water to gently compact it, then level it by dragging a rake back or a screed across the surface, as described in Option 1, above.

Figure 10 shows a side view of flexible foundation of sand only.

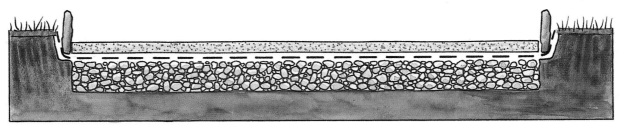

FIGURE 9 **Side view of a flexible foundation of rock and sand**

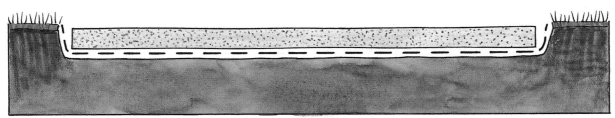

FIGURE 10 **Side view of a flexible foundation of sand only**

your foundation, so the top of your edging material will be flush with any lawn area (so mowing is easy) or just above the surrounding ground. Add a 1-inch (2.5 cm) sand setting bed and (before laying your paving material), set your edging and level it (adjusting the setting bed as necessary). Use a rubber mallet to tap the edging pieces firmly into place, and backfill around them until they're stable. For extra-strong edging, you can substitute 3 to 4 inches (7.6 to 10.2 cm) of wet concrete for the sand setting bed.

■ Modern reproductions of traditional Victorian molded clay edging units will give your floor a more ornamental edge. Install them the same way you would brick edging.

■ Pressure-treated timber edging contrasts nicely with most paving materials. One option is to lay 2 x 4s on edge in trenches deep enough that the top of the wood will be flush with the paved floor (you don't need a sand setting bed; you can lay the 2 x 4s directly on the trench's soil). Make sure the trenches are also wide enough to accommodate 2 x 2 stakes on the outside of the edging to hold it in place. Set the stakes about every 4 feet (1.2 m), with their tops below the surface, then backfill to cover them up. Another option is to set 4 x 4 timbers in edging trenches, drill ⅝-inch (1.6 cm) holes in the timbers about every 4 feet (1.2 m), and drive 2-foot (.6 m) lengths of #5 rebar through each hole and into the foundation to hold them in place (making sure the tops of the rebar lengths are flush with the timber). Heavy, unsawn logs make appealingly rustic edging, especially for floors of gravel and rock. They're also weighty enough that you can simply lay them on well-compacted ground.

■ Finally, if you need the stability of edging but don't like the idea of visible trim, preformed metal and plastic edging will do the job while remaining hidden underground. These are the only types of edging you install after your floor is in place. For details, see page 115.

adding edging

In some cases, you've got to add edging to hold your floor together physically (to contain the pebbles, for example, or to keep the bricks you set on sand from shifting out of place). In others, the main job of edging is to pull everything together visually (often giving a floor a more finished and unified look).

Either way, you've got lots of choices.

■ Many paving materials, including bricks, tiles, stones, and small concrete pavers, make equally effective edging. They also offer the most versatile design options; most can be set on edge, side-by-side, or on end at a diagonal, and smaller pavers work well on curved edges. Excavate the edging trench around

PHOTO 15 **Dry laying pavers, adjusting the sand setting bed underneath, as necessary**

Option 3: Concrete Foundation

If you want a very long-lasting and absolutely level floor, you can't beat a concrete foundation. It won't settle or shift, and it provides an even, finished surface for dry laying or mortaring in place your paving material. It's also quite a bit more labor intensive. The process is the same as pouring a concrete floor, except that you don't have to go to the trouble of finishing the surface, since you'll cover it with sand or mortar and your paving material. Turn to page 124 for step-by-step instructions.

laying your paving material

You've got three basic options for putting in your paving material, as well. Whichever you choose, you'll need to adapt the technique somewhat, depending on the material you're working with. We've outlined each approach here, then provided detailed instructions for laying each type of paving material in the chapters that follow.

PHOTO 16 **Checking the slope of the pavers**

Option 1: Dry Laying

With this simplest of paving options, you place your pavers directly on the foundation's sand setting bed, sweep additional sand into the joints between the pavers, and (despite the technique's name), lightly spray your new floor with water to compact the added sand and flush away any excess. You may need to repeat the process a couple of times, until the sand is well packed and the pavers are firmly set (photos 15 through 18).

PHOTO 17 **Sweeping sand into the joints**

PHOTO 18 **Spraying the floor to compact the setting bed**

You can dry lay on either a flexible foundation or on a concrete foundation to which you've added an inch (2.5 cm) or so of sand. And dry laying is the method to use if you want to plant in the joints between your pavers; just sweep in topsoil rather than sand.

Option 2: Mortaring on a Flexible Foundation

Mortaring your floor on a flexible foundation gives it a more finished appearance and some added stability. (Be sure to use the foundation option that includes crushed rock—at least 4 inches [10.2 cm] of it—it will help prevent the mortar from cracking.) The technique is essentially the same as dry laying, but the finishing ingredient is different. Rather than sweeping sand into the joints between your pavers, you sweep in dry mortar mix. Once the mortar is evenly distributed, spray the floor with water to soak the mix, wait approximately 15 minutes, then spray it again. After the floor is dry and the mortar has hardened, you may need to repeat the process to firmly set all of your pavers. (A note of caution: though this method is much easier than installing a concrete foundation and laying pavers in mortar on top of it, it's also not as durable, and your mortar may eventually crack.)

To create a standard mortar mix, combine one part Portland cement with three parts dry, fine sand.

FIGURE 11 **Coating a concrete slab with outdoor epoxy**

Option 3: Mortaring on a Concrete Foundation

Whether you've poured a concrete foundation for an extra-sturdy floor or you've got a plain concrete patio slab you want to dress up, here's how to mortar your pavers on top of it.

1 If you're working with an existing slab, clean it first with a commercial cleaner or a mix of one part trisodium phosphate (TSP) to five parts water. Scrub the slab with a heavy brush or broom, rinse it, and let it dry.

2 If you're laying thin pavers, such as tile, use a trowel to coat a section of the concrete surface with a thin layer of outdoor epoxy (figure 11). Work on only one manageable section at a time. (A 10-foot-square [3 m] section is about right.)

tip

When you're laying pavers, don't kneel on the ones you've just set to work on the next row; you'll risk upsetting the level surface you worked to establish. Instead, use a scrap of wood on the foundation's sand as a kneeling board. Place it just behind the row you're laying, and work from there.

If you're using heavier pavers, use a mason's trowel to spread a ½ to ¾-inch (1.3 to 1.9 cm) layer of mortar on the concrete, again working on only one manageable section (figure 12). You can use ready-mix mortar (which comes dry by the bag with instructions for adding water). Or, you can mix your own, using a hoe to stir together one part Portland cement and three parts fine sand. Use a sturdy wheelbarrow as your mixing container, and add water (about 2 to 2½ gallons [7.6 to 9.5 L] per bag of cement) until your mix has the consistency of soft mud. It helps to add half of the sand first, then the cement, and then the rest of the sand before adding the water. Use a screed to level the mortar.

3 Lay your pavers on either the epoxy or the mortar, tap each one with a mallet to level it, then let the area rest overnight (figure 13). If you're laying out a precise pattern of brick, tile, or cut stone, you may want to use spacers between each paver to ensure that your spacing is uniform. You can cut your own plywood spacers to place between bricks, then remove them before you grout the joints. For tile or cut stone, you may want to purchase plastic spacers that fit in the corners of each joint. In most cases, you can mortar the joints (step 4) right over the plastic spacers.

FIGURE 12 **Spreading mortar on a concrete slab**

FIGURE 13 **Laying pavers on epoxy or mortar**

keeping it straight

If you want your pavers to form a precise pattern, you need a guide that keeps you from laying crooked rows. Stretch a straight and level line of string across the edge of where you're working, and use it to keep everything in line.

FIGURE 14 **Filling joints with mortar**

4 For mortaring the joints, again you can purchase commercial mortar or mix your own, using a recipe of one part Portland cement and three parts mortar sand. You can also add tinting agents (available in powder form at home-and-building supply stores) to color your mortar so it better matches or accents your pavers. Add water until the mixture is spreadable. Use a trowel (a small pointed trowel works well) or a grout bag to fill the floor's joints with mortar (figure 14). As you work, use a damp sponge to immediately clean any misplaced mortar from the surfaces of your pavers. Once the mortar begins to set (you can tell because it will hold the impression of your finger), finish it off by pulling a jointing tool across it to compact and shape it (figure 15). A thin copper tube makes an excellent jointing tool.

FIGURE 15 **Compacting and shaping the joints to finish them**

planting in the gaps

Plants in the pockets, crevices, and joints of your garden floor are a delightful way to blur lines, making your floor less of a separate landscape element and more an extension of the garden itself.

Planting Steps

■ Fill gaps where you want to add plants with a mixture of equal parts sand and topsoil (plus some compost for added nutrients).

■ Transplant seedlings or sow seeds into the mixture.

■ Water the seeds or transplanted seedlings well and shade transplants for a few days.

■ Mulch the young plants with pine needles or shredded hardwood mulch for several weeks until they're established.

Design Tips

■ If your paved area is spacious and in danger of appearing featureless, open up holes in the paving (by removing pavers or breaking up sections of paving), fill the holes with a soil-and-sand mixture, and set in plants or sow seeds.

■ Use strategically placed plants to help soften the appearance of a floor that looks more formal than you'd like or to add a wonderful contrast of color and texture.

■ Tight positioning helps plants in gaps fill in more quickly, and it gives weeds less of a chance to get established.

Planting in the Gaps boxes throughout the book offer suggestions on plants that do well in various garden floor settings.

brick floors

B rick is one of the most evocative materials you can use to pave your garden floor. Whether the warm, sun-baked surfaces of these familiar clay pavers bring to mind Italian piazzas, college quads, or a favorite grandparent's backyard, for most of us, brick represents something pleasing and enduring. Happily, these adaptable paving modules come in such a broad range of color, texture, and finish that you can use them to bring to life nearly any image they conjure up.

special tools & supplies

You may need to trim your brick pavers to help them conform to the edges of your floor, especially if the edges curve or if you're laying your bricks in a pattern that runs diagonally. You can either hire a masonry professional to help, or use the following tools to make the cuts yourself.

- Pencil or chalk for marking cuts

- Power masonry saw or brick cutter (if you've got lots of cuts to make) or a brick sett (a wide-bladed chisel) and a hammer (if you need to trim only a few pavers)

- Eye and ear protection (for using power equipment)

In addition, if you're installing a flexible base with crushed rock, you may want to rent a power compactor, which will help you create a firmer base.

design options

Traditional patterns used for laying brick are known as bonds. A few of the best loved and most widely used are shown in figure 1. Some bonds create a sense of movement. Others have a much more fixed and formal feel. And fortunately, none come with rules that say you can't mix, match, adapt, or change your paving pattern mid-floor. Combining more than one brick color or incorporating other paving materials can help you emphasize aspects of your paving pattern or add original accents to your overall design.

In addition to the paving pattern you choose, how closely you lay the bricks together and what you use to fill the joints in between will affect your floor's character. Crisp, new bricks laid with tight joints—or mortared with a stark, contrasting color—might make a very formal front drive, for example. Weathered pavers laid with wide gaps filled with topsoil and herbs, on the

PREVIOUS PAGE
Brick doesn't have to be laid in a tidy pattern—or any pattern at all. In this quaint garden-pond surround, whole and broken pavers mix randomly with fieldstones. And forget tight mortaring; grass fills the joints in between.

LEFT **An alternating circular pattern of brick blends with the curved fieldstone wall and rounded bluestone steps beyond**

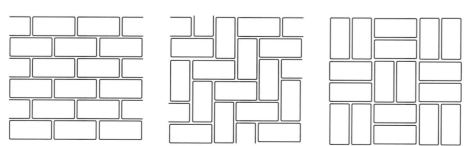

FIGURE 1 **Common brick laying patterns include, left to right, running bond, herringbone, and basketweave.**

garden floor traditions

Centuries ago, granite pavers, cobbles, and bricks were the workhorses of the paving world, providing surfaces for pedestrian streets like this one at Oxford University in England (upper left) and old-world city lanes (upper right). Today, salvaged pavers from similar sites are often given new life in the form of garden floors.

This elegant pool surround of local brick (left) is part of the Generalife Gardens in Granada, Spain. The gardens, which border the Alhambra, a well-known fortress, were built in the 14th century.

ABOVE **Brick in a traditional herringbone pattern**

FACING PAGE **This floor-within-a-floor look is actually a clever expansion of an existing brick patio.**

Finally, your edging choice will figure into your design, too. If you're dry laying your brick on a flexible base, you'll want an edge to help stabilize your floor. Edging isn't as critical if you're mortaring on a concrete base, but you can still add it as a decorative feature. If you're laying your brick beside asphalt (a driveway, for example), an edge in between will be critical. Asphalt tends to settle more than brick. Without a band of edging in between, that settling will create a messy and hazardous ridge.

installation: flexible foundation

other hand, could be perfect for a seating area near the potting shed. When you're choosing the brick itself, you'll also want to consider how well the color and style will blend with brick on surrounding structures.

Foundation

Clear and grade your site, mark your floor layout, and prepare one of the two flexible foundation options described in Chapter 4, page 42. As you calculate the depth of your foundation, plan for your brick surface to end up about ½ to 1 inch (1.3 to 2.5 cm) above the surrounding grade; the elevation will help with the floor's drainage. If you're laying a very informal and small floor, you can get by with the simpler, sand-only foundation (Option 2). For most brick floors, however, you'll want the sturdier foundation of rock and sand (Option 1). Increase the layer of crushed rock in the foundation to 6 to 8 inches (15.2 to 20.3 cm) if your floor is part of an entryway drive or some other area that will need to bear the load of vehicles as well as foot traffic.

purchasing tips

■ Purchase bricks that are low in soluble salts, and they'll be less susceptible to efflorescence, a whitish surface stain caused by salts leaching from the brick or surrounding areas.

■ Specify that you want paving bricks, which are designed to withstand winter freezing and thawing.

■ For bricks that resist chipping and help direct water flow into the floor's foundation, specify chamfered bricks, which are beveled on each edge.

Setting Bed

The top layer of leveled sand in the foundation serves as your setting bed.

Laying the Brick

Begin by stretching level string lines across your floor area to use as guides for keeping your pattern lines straight and your surface level (see page 50). Then, start at one of your floor's outer edges, and lay a small section of brick (about 4 to 5 feet square [1.2 to 1.5 square m]), following your pattern. The size of the joints between the bricks can vary according to your design, but for a traditional-looking floor, you'll want a gap of about 1/16 to 1/8 inch (1.6 to 3 mm). Adjust the sand setting bed underneath, as necessary, to make sure the tops of the bricks are up against the string level. After laying each row, lay a short length of 2 x 4 across the bricks, and tap it to level them. Use a rubber mallet to level individual bricks, if necessary.

Continue laying the rest of your floor the same way. Always kneel in the sand behind where you're working, so you won't dislodge the bricks you've just set in place. And check your work occasionally with a level to make sure you're maintaining the slope you established when you graded your site.

Joints

After laying all the bricks, sprinkle clean, fine, dry sand across the surface of your floor, sweep it into the joints with a stiff push broom, and use a hose to sprinkle the floor lightly with water to settle the sand. Repeat the sweeping-and-watering process until the sand is well packed, the joints are full, and the bricks don't wobble.

Variation

If you've laid your floor on a sturdy foundation of at least 4 inches (10.2 cm) of crushed rock, rather than sweeping sand into the joints between your bricks, you can sweep in dry mortar mix. Once the mortar is evenly distributed, spray the

ABOVE **A simple, circular brick floor helps set off a focal point and connect this garden's paths.**

FACING PAGE **Salvaged bricks mortared tightly together in a basket-weave pattern create the floor for this outdoor retreat.**

floor lightly with water to soak the mix, wait approximately 15 minutes, then spray it again. After the floor is dry and the mortar has hardened, you may need to repeat the process to firmly set all of your bricks. (A note of caution: though this method is much easier than installing a concrete foundation and laying bricks in mortar on top of it, it's also not as durable, and your mortar may eventually crack.)

cutting brick

Cutting large quantities of brick (for a herringbone pattern, for example) is a job best tackled with a power masonry saw or brick cutter and the assistance of someone with experience using the equipment. But if you want to cut a few bricks yourself, you can do it with a brick sett (a wide-bladed chisel) and a hammer. Wearing eye protection, mark the cut line on your paver, place the chisel on the mark, tap the chisel with the hammer to score the line, then strike the chisel with more force to make the final cut. You can finish by using the chisel to lightly smooth any rough edges along the cut. It's a good idea not to cut a brick you're using for paving into pieces less than one-third the brick's original size. Tinier pieces will too easily dislodge from their paved position.

installation: concrete foundation

It involves more work and more expense, but for a crisper look and unquestioning stability, you can lay your brick floor on a concrete foundation.

Foundation

Clear and grade your site, mark your floor layout, and prepare the concrete foundation (Option 3) described in Chapter 4, page 47. Make sure you have installed the expansion joints properly, or you'll get cracking later. Finish the foundation with a rough texture, using a screed or a float, and let it cure for at least seven days before adding the brick.

Setting Bed

You can add ½ to 1 inch (1.3 to 2.5 cm) of sand on top of the concrete foundation, screed it to level it, then dry lay your bricks in the sand, as described above. Or, for ultimate stability, you can lay your bricks in a bed of mortar. For the mortar setting bed, use a mason's trowel to spread a ½ to ¾ inch (1.3 to 1.9 cm) layer of mortar over one workable section of the foundation at a time (about 5 square feet [1.5 square m]).

BELOW **Brick works especially well with other paving materials. Here, it's combined with stones embedded in concrete.**

FACING PAGE **Here, formal planting beds were incorporated into the paving design, making garden and floor one and the same.**

T O P **A 29-foot (9 m) brick runner leading to larger rugs in the garden of Kerr and her husband, artist Robert Richenburg.**

M I D D L E *Peace Offering*, **based on a traditional prayer rug, in a quiet glade below Kerr's studio**

B O T T O M *Flowering Earth*, **designed for its place in this residential flower garden**

weaving tapestries of brick

You never know where laying brick will lead.

Artist Margaret Kerr spent most of the summer of 1986 designing and constructing wide herringbone brick paths for her East Hampton, New York, herb garden. By the time she finished, she had begun to think of bricks—with their warmth, their subtle color variations, and the different textures of their flats and sides—as material for sculpture. And what this lover and collector of Oriental carpets and Middle Eastern tribal floor coverings decided to sculpt were site-specific installations she calls rugs.

Kerr works with a mason to have bricks cut in a wide variety of shapes and sizes. She then plays with combinations to create intricate geometric patterns and uses natural variations in brick texture and color to add accents such as borders and fringe. Some of her works are based on specific rugs. Most are simply inspired by her years of study of rug design, with patterns emerging as she moves bricks around in the sand. She creates on-site installations, laying the brick on compacted stone dust or sand and edging it with concrete. She also makes portable rugs, which are laid in sand in a specially designed steel frame, then transported from her studio to their garden homes, where they're installed intact into the ground.

RIGHT **This tiny tree surround is made of handmade Sussex brick laid in a bed of crushed flint, in which pockets were opened up and planted with thyme.**

Mortar sets quickly, so you don't want to apply it to the entire foundation at once. Screed the mortar to level it. If your brick pavers are especially thin, apply an epoxy coat to the concrete prior to spreading on the mortar, then add only ½ inch (1.3 cm) of mortar.

Laying the Brick

Press the bricks into the mortar according to your design, placing spacers between each to keep the spacing even (typically about ⅜ inch [9.5 mm]). You can either place the bricks onto the mortar and add more mortar between the joints later after they've set, or you can "butter" one end and one side of each brick with mortar before laying it. As you set each one, lightly tap it with a mallet to settle it. After laying each row, lay a short length of 2 x 4 across the bricks, and tap it to level them. It's a good idea to keep a bucket of water and a piece of burlap nearby. Dampened burlap is a good tool for rubbing off any mortar that makes its way to the surface of a brick. Continue laying the rest of your bricks, then let the floor rest overnight.

Joints

Use a small pointed trowel or a grout bag to fill the joints between the bricks with mortar. If you used the "buttering" method for laying your bricks, you'll simply be filling in any spots that aren't completely full. (This is another good time to keep a piece of burlap and water handy, to immediately clean any misplaced mortar from the surfaces of your bricks.) Once the mortar begins to set (you can tell because it will hold the impression of your finger), finish it off by pulling a jointing tool across it to compact and shape it.

Let your newly mortared floor settle for a day before walking on it. A week later, brush the surface with a stiff brush to clean up stray mortar drips and dust.

Maintenance

If you dry lay your brick on sand, individual pavers will dislodge or settle in too deeply now and then. Use a flat-headed screwdriver to remove problem pavers, adjust (and in many cases add to) the sand underneath, then position the brick back in place. Occasionally, you'll also need to replace washed-out sand in the joints between bricks and do a bit of weeding.

Efflorescence, the whitish mineral that leaches out of brick, creating stains or streaks, won't compromise the strength of your floor, but it can be unattractive. If it doesn't disappear with normal weathering, choose a warm, dry day to wash it off with water and a rag, or brush it away with a stiff, dry brush. In the winter, choose a rubber-tipped shovel for removing snow from your brick floor; metal shovels will chip the brick, and de-icing chemicals and rock salt will discolor it.

tile
floors

If your garden environment is in need of a tad more flair, tile paving could give it just the lift you're looking for. Colorful glazed tiles invoke images of outdoor floors surrounding ancient Persian pools. Configure the tiles into a mosaic pattern, and your new patio will look as if it was plucked from a traditional Moroccan garden. Or, choose rough, sun-drenched terra-cotta tile, and you can create a terrace with the stark beauty of a desert setting. Whether you want warmth, color, regional flavor, or humor and whimsy, incorporating this adaptable paving material is one of the most effective ways to add character to your garden setting.

LEFT **A terrace paved with tiles of different sizes, shapes, and colors**

PREVIOUS PAGE **A classic-looking entranceway paved with basic terra-cotta tiles**

special tools & supplies

◾ Tile cutter and/or a wet saw (You may need to trim your tiles to help them conform to your laying pattern or to the edges of your floor. A tile cutter is good for straight cuts. Rent a wet saw for making curved or angled cuts.)

◾ Notched trowel (This tool with a flat bottom and a toothed comb on the sides is perfect for preparing a mortar setting bed for tile.)

◾ Rubber-faced grout float (for spreading grout into your floor's joints)

◾ Power compactor (If you're installing a flexible base with crushed rock, you may want to rent a power compactor, which will help you create a firmer base.)

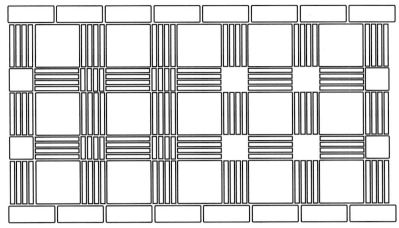

FIGURE 1 **Flat tiles surrounded by tiles laid on edge. For added effect, you can inset smaller flat tiles at the corner joints.**

BELOW **Bluestone pavers edged with unglazed tile joints and glazed tile inserts**

design options

You can achieve a whole lot of effect with tile—without a lot of tile. Sure, you can pave an entire patio with 12-inch (30.5 cm) squares of earth-toned terra-cotta and end up with a handsomely textured floor. But you can also scatter inserts of randomly sized patterned tiles among sandstone pavers, embed cut pieces of glazed tile into a poured concrete slab, or create a small tiled focal point within a floor paved with another material. Because tile pavers come in a range of sizes and they're fairly easy to reshape by cutting, they lend themselves to more intricate laying patterns than most other materials. (Flipping through books that feature photos of centuries-old tile floors in warm, sunny climates around the world can be a wonderful source of inspiration.) One especially interesting pattern, traditionally laid with slate, is to surround flat tiles by tiles set on edge (see figure 1).

The type of tile you choose will also affect
the tone of your design. Machine-shaped
tiles, with their crisp, uniform edges, will
have a more contemporary look, while
hand-molded tiles, which will vary slightly
from paver to paver, tend to have a more
rustic appearance.

installation

Foundation

Clear and grade your site, mark your floor
layout, and prepare the concrete foundation (Option 3) described in Chapter 4,
page 47. (Tiles are too thin to lay on a
flexible foundation; they need firmer support to prevent them from cracking under
the pressure of feet and furniture.) Make
sure you incorporate expansion joints into
the concrete foundation (again, to prevent
future cracking). Finish the foundation
with a rough texture, using a screed or a
float, and let it cure for at least seven days
before adding the tile.

LEFT The various understated shades of glazed quarry tile in this terrace do a nice job of matching the nearby brick without upstaging all the surrounding blooms.

garden floor traditions

Gardens in Moorish Spain were often divided by tiled walkways, with a fountain or a kiosk where the walkways crossed. This 12th-century garden floor in Málaga, Spain (Moorish Alcazar), features tiles and insets of contrasting colors of pebbles. It's edged with brick and bluestone.

Setting Bed

Again, a sand setting bed won't provide enough stability for tile; you should lay your tile pavers on a bed of latex-Portland cement mortar. Dampen the concrete foundation, then use the flat side of a notched trowel to spread a ¼ to ⅜-inch-thick (6 to 9.5 mm) layer of the mortar over one workable section of the foundation at a time (about 5 square feet [1.5 square m]). (Mortar sets quickly, so you don't want to apply it to the entire foundation at once.) With the notched side of the trowel, comb the mortar, holding the trowel at a 45° angle to the foundation.

Laying the Tile

Press the tiles into place on the combed mortar. Use tile spacers (available from most masonry suppliers) in the joints if you want uniform spaces between each paver. When you set the tiles, do so gently. You don't want the mortar filling more than one-third of the depth of the joints.

If your tiles have textured backs, you may want to coat their backs with grout before laying them. The grout coating will ensure full mortar coverage, with no voids to collect water that can freeze and cause your tiles to crack.

After laying each row, lay a short length of 2 x 4 across the tiles, and tap each lightly with a mallet to settle and level it. It's a good idea to keep a bucket of water and a sponge nearby, so you can quickly sponge off any mortar that makes its way to the surface of a tile. Continue laying the rest of your tiles, then let the floor rest overnight.

cutting tile

Rent a tile cutter from a masonry supplier, and making simple, straight cuts will be a snap. First, you position the tile in the cutter's metal frame and draw its carbide-tipped blade or wheel across the tile to score it. Then, you simply press down on the cutter's handle until the tile breaks cleanly along the score line. For more intricate cuts, either hire a masonry professional to help, or, if you have some experience using the equipment, rent a wet saw.

Joints

The following day, remove all your tile spacers (or leave them in and grout over them). Dampen the tiles, and spread a commercial tile grout mix over the surface, preparing and applying the mix according to the manufacturer's instructions. Push the grout into the joints with a rubber-faced grout float, let it set for the manufacturer's recommended amount of time (typically about 15 minutes), then wipe the tile faces clean with a damp sponge. Let the grout dry for the second

BELOW In this radiant setting, unglazed tile blends beautifully with poured concrete, concrete blocks, flagstones, and bright decorative tile.

LEFT **Terra-cotta tiles were cut in squares and filler strips to surround this curved planter.**

recommended amount of time (about 40 minutes), wipe off the tiles with a soft, dry cloth, then cover the floor with plastic and let it damp cure for three to seven days.

Maintenance

Tiles mortared on a concrete foundation will be pretty firmly set and won't require much maintenance, though individual tiles may crack and need to be replaced.

planting in the gaps: *moss*

If your floor is in a shady spot, moss can be an especially picturesque plant for carpeting the gaps between the pavers.

Growing moss yourself is a bit of a challenge, but you can transplant sections from construction sites, drainage ditches, or anyplace where high-acid soil has been compacted and neglected. (Collect moss that is already wet—after a good rain is the best time.) Prepare the gaps where you want the moss to go by pulling up all existing growth and watering until the soil is muddy. Spray the moss patches, then gently press them into the wet gaps. You can carefully stretch the moss to fit the gaps, then fill any remaining open places with soil.

Moss has no roots or veins (it must absorb water from where it grows), so be sure to water it lightly but frequently until it's established. You won't need to mulch it in the winter, but you might want to apply a solution of one part dried skim milk or buttermilk and seven parts water twice a day for two weeks in the spring to repair any winter damage and help acidify the soil.

ornamental
gravel & pebble
floors

Gravel and pebbles—the least complicated of paving materials—are also among the most venerable. The ancient Greeks used pebble paving for both indoor and outdoor floors. The Japanese raked gravel into symbolic patterns in meditation gardens and paved the banks of their pond gardens with round pebbles. And the Moors used small stones in shades of gray, white, and purplish blue to create mosaic floors featuring intricate patterns. What a relief to have all that tradition to back you up! You can confidently use gravel or pebbles today, whether you want a formal floor to frame your parterre garden or a comfy patch of paved ground near your herb beds.

design options

When you're planning a floor of gravel or pebbles, much of the design work is in the choosing of the material. With options including dark polished river stones, honey-colored gravel, stark-white angular chippings, and many other variations, gravel and pebbles become the raw ingredients for looks ranging from rustic to urban, old-world to contemporary. Gravel and pebbles also blend easily with other paving materials and landscaping elements, whether you want to wrap your gravel floor around an existing tree or fill extra-large joints between pavers with colored pebbles. Edge restraints are a good idea with gravel or small stones that might otherwise migrate from the garden floor to the grass beyond; consider incorporating the edging into your overall design. Though simple steel edging, which is nearly unnoticeable, will do the job, other materials, such as brick, stone, and timber, keep your gravel in place while adding to the floor's character.

BELOW For centuries, small stones have been used to create floor mosaics and other interesting patterns for outdoor floor designs. For details on embedding pebbles in concrete, see page 132.

installation

Foundation

On a site that drains well, you can use a simpler, modified version of the flexible foundation (Option 1) described in Chapter 4, page 42. Excavate the foundation to a depth of 3 inches (7.6 cm), and add a trench around the foundation for your edging material. Fill the foundation with 2 inches (5.1 cm) of road bond, the unscreened gravel described on page 42,

featuring lots of granite dust and small particles that compact into a strong yet flexible base. Compact the road bond well. You may need to add additional road bond after compacting, to bring your foundation layer up to its full 2 inches (5.1 cm). Once your foundation is set, install your edging material.

If drainage is a problem, excavate your foundation 7 to 8 inches (17.8 to 20.3 cm), lay a 1-inch (2.5 cm) layer of crushed rock, then install a 4-inch (10.2 cm) perforated PVC pipe, holes facing down, and direct

BELOW **A simple gravel floor is an un-obtrusive backdrop for this serene garden setting.**

FACING PAGE **This imaginative pat-terned floor is made of alternating blocks of river stone and brick**

RIGHT Gravel provides the perfect floor for this outdoor living room.

it to a low area where it can release water. Wrap the pipe with landscape fabric or a specially designed landscape sock, to keep it from getting clogged with sediment. Finally, fill the rest of the foundation with another 6 to 7 inches (15.2 to 17.8 cm) of crushed rock.

Adding the Gravel or Pebbles

Simply add your top layer of paving material to the remaining 1 inch (2.5 cm) of space in your foundation. Shovel it onto the foundation, rake it, spray it lightly with water, then tamp it to settle it. Once tamped, your gravel or pebble layer should sit about 1 inch (2.5 cm) below the top edge of the surrounding ground, so it won't be likely to spill out past your floor's borders.

BELOW Often, gravel doesn't have to take center stage to add interesting texture to a garden floor.

maintenance

You may want to rake your gravel or pebble floor occasionally to neaten it up. Every once in awhile, you'll also want to hoe out weeds and pick out any debris, such as fallen leaves from surrounding trees. Unless your new floor gets heavy use, it will likely be years before you need to replenish the surface layer.

ABOVE **Add it to a carefully planned garden design, and gravel can become the most formal of paving materials.**

RIGHT **Gravel floors must be contained with an edging. Here, cobbles do the job.**

BELOW **In this Japanese-style garden gravel makes a natural bed for rough stones.**

purchasing tip

If you want the ease and low cost of a gravel or pebble floor, but you also want your surface to be accessible to wheels (whether in the form of strollers or wheelchairs), consider using granite fines, also called rock dust, instead of gravel. Granite fines create a smooth, stable surface that is both handicap accessible and easier for someone wearing high heels to negotiate. If you go with granite fines, use a power compactor to prepare your foundation and to compact the fines, so you're sure your floor is as firm as possible. It's best to use fines on a flatter or only slightly sloped site, otherwise gullies will form in your floor surface when it rains.

Dry stream beds make a wonderful foundation for adding a winding strip of decorative paving to a garden. Here, gardeners have added blue glass and stepping stones (LEFT) and multiple colors of smoothed stones (BELOW).

garden floor traditions

In the 11th century, Buddhist monks introduced the concept of Zen gardens in Japan. First located primarily in the courtyards of monasteries and temples, these symbolic combinations of raked gravel, large boulders, and manicured patches of vegetation have become a garden style used around the world. The three shown on the right , located in Kyoto, Japan, date to the 17th century.

A B O V E **Cut stone and decorative pebbles edge the moss floor of this 16th-century temple garden, also in Kyoto, Japan.**

flagstone
& fieldstone

With their delightful assortment of bumps, nicks, irregularities, and ragged edges, these unpretentious stones can create garden floors that look as if they grew up—slowly and comfortably—right out of their surroundings. Most accessible and affordable (not to mention most appealing if you're after a natural look) will be stones that have been gathered or quarried in your local area, whether that means indigenous limestone or quarried rough marble. Their subtle, changing shades and distinctive textures will reflect the character of your region—and gently link your garden with the larger landscape.

special tools & supplies

When laying flagstone or fieldstone, you've often got to do some trimming here and there, shaping the pieces so they fit together. To do so, you'll need the following:

- Pencil or chalk for marking cuts
- Mason's chisel and hammer
- Eye protection

design options

With flagstone and fieldstone, you won't be able to plot your paving pattern exactly, as you can with brick, for example. But you can make some design choices in advance, starting with the stones you pick. Think about whether you want stones that are relatively similar in size and shape: all smallish fieldstones with rounded edges, maybe, or huge flagstones in rough rectangular shapes. Or, maybe you'd rather your look be more random, with a mix of

ABOVE **Mortared brick makes a tidy edge for flagstone floors that you want to look a bit less casual. This one makes space for a central focal point surrounded by plantings.**

FACING PAGE **Broken units of lilac bluestone blend artfully with the stacked-stone wall that borders the floor.**

LEFT Flagstone lends itself to a number of landscaping elements. Use it as a paving material, and your floor can blend seamlessly with benches, fire pits, and walls like the one shown here.

LOWER LEFT Coordinating colors of brick and flagstone are combined to create this multilevel patio area.

sizes, shapes, and even colors of stones. Consider, too, the option of combining the stones with other paving materials; brick and gravel are two of the most common companions. What you use to fill the joints between the stones will also affect your floor's character. Mortar will make it neater and more polished, sand or soil will look less formal, and plantings in the joints will give your floor an always-been-there air. Edging isn't necessary for the uneven edges of these stone floors, but you can add it as a purely decorative element if you want your floor to look a bit more finished.

installation: flexible foundation

Foundation

Clear and grade your site, mark your floor layout, and prepare one of the two flexible foundation options described in Chapter 4, page 42. If you're laying a very informal floor and using only large and thick stones, you can get by with

planting in the gaps:
full sun

A starter list of tolerant, hardy plants you can incorporate into soil-filled gaps of a garden floor that gets a lot of light:

Baby's Breath (*Gypsophilia repens*). Clusters of small pink or white flowers on thin stems.

Harebell (*Campanula rotundifolia*). Broad, bell-shaped blue flowers in late summer.

Lady's Mantle (*Alchemilla mollis*). Gray-green leaves, chartreuse flowers in the summer.

Moss Phlox (*Phlox subulata*). Creeping stems with needle-like evergreen leaves. Early summer flowers range from white, pink, and rose to lavender blue.

Sandwort (*Arenaria montana*). Blooms white from late spring to early summer. Needs moist soil in full sun.

Sedum, dwarf types. Low, drought-tolerant plants with carpet-like foliage and flowers. They're not as resilient as others, though. Plant them on the edges of floors; they won't survive heavy traffic.

Snow-in-Summer (*Cerastium tomentosum*). Gray leaves with white flowers in early summer. Needs soil that drains well.

Thyme, albus and wooly (*Thymus pseudolanuginosus* and *Thymus praecox*). Wooly thyme features silver-gray mats and lavender flowers. With albus thyme, you'll have emerald green mats and white flowers.

the simpler, sand-only foundation (Option 2) or even lay the stones directly on the ground—just excavate a small amount of soil to make a spot for them, and let grass or other plants grow in between the pavers. For most other flagstone and fieldstone floors, you'll want the sturdier foundation of rock and sand (Option 1). If you're paving your floor with small stones only, use road bond in place of the rock in the foundation for added stability (this alternative is described on page 42), or prepare a concrete foundation (see page 97).

ABOVE **The wider-than-usual gaps between stones in this picturesque floor break traditional paving rules—let's hear it for rebellion!**

ABOVE **A casual outdoor carpet of broken flagstone and baby's tears**

LEFT **Fieldstones creating a drainage channel in a flagstone floor**

tip

Use topsoil instead of sand between the joints if you want to set in creeping plants.

Setting Bed

The top layer of leveled sand in the foundation serves as your setting bed.

Laying the Stone

The fun of laying irregular stone is that it's much more like piecing together a puzzle than following a formula. There's an added challenge, though: these puzzle pieces are often heavy. The process will flow more smoothly as you develop an eye for which stones will fit best where, without having to move each one in and out of place multiple times.

Begin at one of your floor's outer edges. If your stones vary in size, place larger ones here and at door thresholds and where paths lead away from the floor, so they can provide added stability. Lay several stones, shaping them with the chisel as necessary, and leaving a gap of about ¼ to ¾ inch (6 mm to 1.9 cm) between them (or larger if you want to plant between the gaps). Once you have several in place where you want them, work each one into the sand, then tap it with a rubber mallet to settle it. Fieldstones, especially, will have uneven thicknesses, so you'll need to adjust the setting bed to help the stones sit level by digging out spots or by filling them in.

Continue laying the rest of your floor the same way, stepping back every now and then to see how it's looking. Always kneel

making a fit

You'll often need to chip, trim, and make outright cuts to get all the pieces of a flagstone floor to fit together just right. With most types of stone, you can make the adjustments yourself with a mason's chisel. Simply nick off small pieces or, for bigger cuts, follow these steps. First, mark your cut line with a pencil or chalk. Then, slip on some eye protection and score the line with the chisel itself or by hitting the chisel with a hammer. Once you've scored the stone, place it on a piece of wood or on another rock, letting the score line and the portion you want to remove overhang, and strike one sharp blow to split it along the score line.

Dense stones such as slate are in danger of shattering if you cut them with a chisel; they respond better to a water-cooled mason's saw (also known as a wet saw) or a circular saw fitted with a diamond blade. If these aren't tools you keep on hand in your own shed, enlist the help of a stonemason for your cutting jobs.

in the sand behind where you're working, so you won't dislodge the stones you've just set in place. And check your work occasionally with a level to make sure you're maintaining the slope you established when you graded your site.

Joints

After laying all the stone, sprinkle clean, fine, dry sand across the surface of your floor, sweep it into the joints with a stiff push broom, and use a hose to sprinkle the floor lightly with water to settle the sand. Repeat the sweeping-and-watering process until the sand is well packed (about ¼ inch [6 mm] below the surface of the stones) and the stones don't wobble.

Variation

If you've laid your floor on a sturdy foundation of at least 4 inches (10.2 cm) of crushed rock, rather than sweeping sand into the joints between your stones, you can sweep in dry mortar mix. Once the

BELOW **This tiny flagstone seating area is an extension of the surrounding garden.**

garden floor traditions

Katsura Imperial Villa in Kyoto, Japan, the country's earliest-known stroll garden, dates to the early 1600s. Stroll gardens are designed as dynamic compositions meant to fluctuate with the seasons, the growth of foliage, and the passage of time. Here, huge slabs of local fieldstone, simply laid in the soil, form a serene and unadorned section of flooring.

mortar is evenly distributed, spray the floor with water to soak the mix, wait approximately 15 minutes, then spray it again. After the floor is dry and the mortar has hardened, you may need to repeat the process to firmly set all of your stones. (A note of caution: though this method is much easier than installing a concrete foundation and laying stones in mortar on top of it, it's also not as durable, and your mortar may eventually crack.)

tip

If the surfaces of your stones are rough and uneven, you may have to rely on a trained eye rather than a level for checking slope. Bend down so your eyes are at nearly ground level, and gauge your floor's slope as best you can.

FACING PAGE
**Filling the joints be-
tween the flagstone
with crushed rock of
a similar shade gives
this floor a neat,
somewhat polished
appearance.**

**LEFT AND
BELOW The
gentle curve of this
mortared flagstone
patio follows the line
of the terraced gar-
dens and rock wall
that surround it.**

installation:
concrete
foundation

A concrete foundation provides maximum stability for any garden floor. If
that's what you're after for your flagstone or fieldstone floor, the procedure
is the same as the one for installing cut
stone on a concrete foundation, outlined on page 105.

maintenance

If you've dry laid your stones on a
flexible foundation, some of them may
occasionally shift out of place as the
floor gets more and more use. Simply
adjust the sand setting bed, as necessary,
to resettle or level them again. You'll
probably also need to add more sand
between the joints every year or so and
do some weeding in the joints now and
then. If you'll be shoveling snow from
your floor during its off season, make
sure your shovel is rubber tipped, so you
avoid chipping or scratching the stone.

cut stone floors

Cut stone, also called ashlar, is the city cousin of flagstone and fieldstone. It's the branch of the family that favors precise forms, uniform sizes, and refined paving patterns. If you want your terrace, poolside patio, or courtyard floor to feature a dash of elegance and formality, this handsome paving material, which includes sandstone, limestone, bluestone, slate, granite, and marble, has the pedigree to pull it off.

PREVIOUS
PAGE **Unmortared
stone slabs mingled
with plants for an infor-
mal floor.**

**Cut stone is an obvious
choice for crisp, formal-
looking floors; mortar
the pavers together with
tight joints for ultimate
polish** (L E F T). **If, however, you want a slightly
softer look, widen the
joints and fill them with
groundcover instead**
(L O W E R   L E F T).

special tools & supplies

You may need to trim your stones to help
them conform to the edges of your floor,
especially if the edges curve or if you're
setting the stones on a diagonal. You can
either hire a masonry professional to help,
or use the following tools to make the cuts
yourself.

 Pencil or chalk for marking stone

Circular saw with masonry blade

Sturdy piece of lumber to use as a cutting guide

Eye and ear protection

In addition, if you're installing a flexible
base with crushed rock, you may want to
rent a power compactor. It'll help you create a firmer base, which you may want if
you're laying a thin, brittle paving stone.

design options

Predictability has its advantages. Once you've settled on the shape and size of the cut stone you'll be using, you can plot your floor design on graph paper rather than by moving actual stones around. Simply make a scaled drawing of your patio area, with 1 inch (2.5 cm) on your paper representing 1 foot (30.5 cm) on the ground. Then, make copies of the drawing (or lay tracing paper on top of it), and play with paving patterns.

Just because individual types of cut stone are uniform in size and shape doesn't mean your design has to be routine. Consider mingling several different forms and even different shades of stone—or eliminating stones altogether in key places and adding other paving materials or plantings. Creeping plants incorporated within the surface or along the edges of a cut stone floor can help soften the design if it becomes too austere. The look of your cut stone floor will also be affected by how tight you make the joints between stones, whether you line them up or offset

ABOVE **A quiet retreat area paved with granite blocks laid with an informal, curved edge. A circular opening in the floor makes room for plantings.**

them (offsetting them makes for a stronger floor), and whether you seed the joints with grass, fill them with a light mortar, or choose something else altogether. Finally, though edging isn't necessary as a restraining edge, you may want to add it for aesthetic appeal.

installation: flexible foundation

Foundation

Clear and grade your site, mark your floor layout, and prepare the sturdier foundation of rock and sand (Option 1) described in Chapter 4, page 42. If the paving stones you've chosen are on the thin side, use road bond in place of the rock in the foundation for added stability (this alternative is described on page 42), or prepare a concrete foundation (see page 105).

Setting Bed

The top layer of leveled sand in the foundation serves as your setting bed.

---

planting in the gaps:
full or partial shade

A starter list of floor plants that can handle a bit of abuse (such as foot traffic), but not full sun:

Bruce's White or Blue Ridge (*Phlox stolonifera*). Low, creeping, woodland plant with white or blue flowers.

Bugleweed (*Ajuga reptans*). Low-to-the-ground plant. Blue, white, or pink flowers in spring.

Bunchberry (*Chamaepericlymenum canadensis*). Formerly known as Cornus canadensis. Tiny clusters of white blossoms in spring followed by red berries. Leaves become burgundy red in the fall.

Foamflower (*Tiarella cordifolia*). Creeping stems, heart-shaped leaves, and white flowers in the spring.

Partridgeberry (*Mitchella repens*). Small evergreen leaves and light pink flowers. Red berries in the fall.

Periwinkle or Myrtle (*Vinca minor*). Trailing, evergreen ground cover with blue or white flowers.

Wintergreen (*Gaultheria procumbens*). Creeping plant with shiny leaves and tiny white flowers followed by scarlet berries.

Strawberry Geranium (*Saxifraga stolonifera*). Creeping plant with white-veined leaves and white flowers that makes runners like strawberries.

Laying the Stone

With your graph-paper design in hand, temporarily lay out a portion of your floor to make sure you're happy with your plan. Once you're satisfied, begin by stretching level string lines across your floor area to use as guides for keeping your pattern lines straight and your surface level (see page 50).

Start at one of your floor's outer edges, and lay several stones. The size of the joints between the stones can vary according to your design, but for a traditional floor, you'll want a gap of about ¼ to ¾ inch (6 mm to 1.9 cm). Adjust the sand setting bed underneath, as necessary, to make sure the tops of the stones are up against the string level. Once you have several stones in place where you want them, tap each with a rubber mallet to settle it.

Continue laying the rest of your floor the same way. Always kneel in the sand behind where you're working, so you won't dislodge the stones you've just set in place. And check your work occasionally with a level to make sure you're maintaining the slope you established when you graded your site.

Joints

After laying all the stone, sprinkle clean, fine, dry sand across the surface of your floor, sweep it into the joints with a stiff push broom, and use a hose to sprinkle

the floor lightly with water to settle the sand. Repeat the sweeping-and-watering process until the sand is well packed (about ¼ inch [6 mm] below the surface of the stones) and the stones don't wobble.

Variation

If you've laid your floor on a sturdy foundation of at least 4 inches (10.2 cm) of crushed rock, rather than sweeping sand into the joints between your stones, you can sweep in dry mortar mix. Once the mortar is evenly distributed, spray the floor with water to soak the mix, wait approximately 15 minutes, then spray it again. After the floor is dry and the mortar has hardened, you may need to repeat the process to firmly set all of your stones. (A note of caution: though this method is

ABOVE **Random cuts of bluestone combined with flag-stone and pea gravel**

RIGHT **Large cut stone pavers are substantial enough to hold their own when combined with a stout rock wall and sturdy furniture.**

LOWER RIGHT **This parking terrace gives visitors their first impression. It's laid with a neat pattern of mortared stones and a decorative brick insert.**

much easier than installing a concrete foundation and laying stones in mortar on top of it, it's also not as durable, and your mortar may eventually crack.)

installation: concrete foundation

The process is more expensive—and it's more work—but mortaring your cut stones in place on top of a concrete foundation gives you a stronger, longer-lasting, and more finished-looking floor.

Foundation

Clear and grade your site, mark your floor layout, and prepare the concrete foundation (Option 3) described in Chapter 4, page 47. Finish it with a rough texture, using a screed or a float, and let it cure for at least seven days before adding the stone.

Setting Bed

With a mason's trowel, spread a ¾ to 1-inch (1.9 to 2.5 cm) layer of mortar over one workable section of the foundation at

a time (about 5 square feet [1.5 square m]). Mortar sets quickly, so you don't want to apply it to the entire foundation at once. Screed the mortar to level it.

Laying the Stone

Begin pressing stones into the mortar according to your design, and tap each with a mallet. If you want the joints between the stones to be uniform, use spacers between each. After you've laid several stones, place a level or a long, straight board over them to make sure they're flat. Adjust any that aren't by

tapping them into place. It's a good idea to keep a bucket of water and a sponge nearby, so you can quickly sponge off any mortar that makes its way to the surface of a stone before the mortar stains it. Continue laying the rest of your stones, then let the floor rest overnight.

Joints

Use a small pointed trowel or a grout bag to fill the joints between the stones with mortar. (This is another good time to keep a sponge and water handy, to immediately clean any misplaced mortar from

BELOW **Brick edging keeps this unmortared table support made of marble slabs in place**

the surfaces of your stones.) Once the mortar begins to set (you can tell because it will hold the impression of your finger), finish it off by pulling a jointing tool across it to compact and shape it.

Maintenance

If you've dry laid your stones on a flexible foundation, you may need to occasionally rework them to keep the surface smooth and level. You'll probably also need to add more sand between the joints every year or so and do some weeding in the joints now and then. Mortared stone on a concrete foundation should require no more maintenance than periodic sweeping. If you'll be using a snow shovel on either during the off season, make it one that's rubber tipped, so you don't scratch the stone.

garden floor traditions

Cutting and shaping stones to create both indoor and outdoor floors is an age-old process used by cultures ranging from the ancient Incas of Peru to the Greeks. Here, an elaborate floor of the Courtyard of Bastille in France features cut stone laid in a scalloped pattern surrounding a larger stone centerpiece.

concrete paver floors

L ittle wonder that concrete pavers have been winning popularity contests with home land-scapers lately. When a material is inexpensive, easy to install, highly durable, and available in a huge range of multipurpose styles, it tends to become a crowd pleaser. To meet the demand, paver suppliers are rapidly expanding their lines. At nearly any home improvement center today, you can find pavers in a wide selection of colors, textures, shapes, and patterns, including concrete pavers that link together in a sturdy interlocking design.

PREVIOUS PAGE Leaving extra-wide gaps for planting between these concrete pavers allows the distinction between garden and floor to blur.

TOP Close-up of a hexagonal paver stamped with an intricate pattern and laid with tight joints

MIDDLE Pavers made to mimic cut limestone

BOTTOM A standard style of interlocking concrete pavers

special tools & supplies

If you're laying your pavers according to a pattern, you may need to trim them here and there to help them conform to the edges of your floor. You can either hire a masonry professional to help, or use the following tools (and the same process you'd use for cutting brick, page 59) to make the cuts yourself.

▪ Pencil or chalk for marking cuts

▪ Power masonry saw (if you've got lots of cuts to make) or a mechanical paver splitter (if you need to trim only a few pavers)

You'll also need a power compactor (a compact base is essential for this material) and eye and ear protection (for using power equipment).

TOP **Irregular cuts allow these concrete pavers to conform to a circular design.**

MIDDLE **Brick-like concrete pavers are available in an array of colors.**

BOTTOM **Pigmented pavers stamped with a wave-like pattern**

design options

Concrete pavers lend themselves to three general types of paving designs.

 Interlocking pavers, made to fit together snugly and create a very sturdy surface, are a good choice for large floor areas such as drives and parking pads that need to be strong enough to bear heavy loads. The result is neat and orderly, but definitely manufactured; if you want a natural effect, interlocking pavers won't suit you.

If you want to imitate the look of nearly any other paving material—cut bluestone, granite block, brick, you name it—there's likely a look-alike concrete paver on the market to help you do it. When you've got a lot of ground to cover, concrete is often far less expensive, more accessible, and easier to work with than the real thing, and good imitations are quite convincing.

making concrete pavers

Okay, it's not the quickest route to paving your garden floor. But making your own pavers, even if you create only a few to place here and there among dozens of other commercial pavers, is one of the best ways to make your floor one of a kind.

1 Start with a cement mixture of 3 parts sand and 1 part cement, then mix in approximately 1 part water, until the cement is a pouring consistency. (You can also add dye at this point, if you want to color your pavers.) Choose or make a plastic mold that's about 2 to 3 inches (5.1 to 7.6 cm) deep and bottomless. The top rim of a large flowerpot works well for round pavers. Home-and-garden stores sell other molds in various shapes. Lubricate the inside of the mold with oil, set it on a sheet of plastic, then fill it to the top with the concrete mixture.

2 Drag a straight edge across the top of the mold to even and level the surface.

3 Decorate the paver by embedding the wet concrete with nearly any durable material you like, from tile fragments and glass nuggets to marbles and pieces of broken ceramic pots. Wearing rubber gloves, press the pieces into place, then push each piece in with a float, so about two-thirds of its depth is embedded. This is a wonderful way to incorporate mementoes from travels (maybe oyster shells from last summer's beach trip), sentimental bits (perhaps the remnants of a shattered piece of your grandmother's china), and other meaningful tokens.

4 When the concrete is dry and fully set (about three days after pouring it), remove the mold by applying pressure and pulling outward around the edge. Finally, use a stiff-bristled brush to remove any excess concrete from the paver's surface, then clean it off with a fine spray of water.

LEFT **Laying a floor doesn't have to be a huge undertaking. Here, a small section of concrete pavers creates a snug seating area just off a gravel path.**

BELOW **Concrete pavers come in a multitude of shapes—and can be simply laid in a bed of decorative stone.**

On the other hand, you may choose concrete pavers simply because they can look appealingly fabricated. If you want to pave your floor with fun geometric shapes, a collection of colors, or personalized pieces (such as pavers that have been painted, stamped, or embedded with designs), you can choose from a delightful selection of commercial pavers—or even make your own.

installation

Foundation

Clear and grade your site, mark your floor layout, and prepare the sturdier foundation of rock and sand (Option 1) described in Chapter 4, page 42. Use at least 4 inches (10.2 cm) of crushed rock in the foundation if you're building a floor that will bear light pedestrian traffic, 6 inches (15.2 cm) for a floor that will be traveled heavily, and 8 inches (20.3 cm) for a driveway. Add the 1-inch (2.5 cm) layer of sand, then wet (but don't saturate) the foundation material with a sprinkler and compact it well.

In most cases, concrete pavers, especially those you'll be laying in a tight or interlocking design, require an edge restraint to hold the floor firmly in place. Be sure to dig a trench around your floor foundation that is deep and wide enough to hold the edging you've chosen.

Setting Bed

The 1-inch (2.5 cm) layer of leveled sand in the foundation serves as your setting bed. Be sure to use clean, washed, coarse concrete sand and not fine mason's sand or silica sand. Screed the sand to level the surface.

Laying the Pavers

How you lay your concrete pavers will depend on which type you've chosen. If you're working with brick-like pavers or those that have an interlocking design, proceed as if you were laying a brick floor. Begin by stretching level string lines across your floor area to use as guides for keeping your pattern lines straight and your surface level (see page 50). Start at one of your floor's outer edges, and lay a small section of pavers (about 4 to 5 feet square [1.2 to 1.5 square m]), following your pattern. If you want a floor with maximum strength, it's best to lay the pavers so the joints are as tight as possible; try to make them no larger than ⅛ inch (3 mm). If you're working with larger pavers, lay

---

hidden metal or plastic edging

Metal and PVC edging, which work especially well with interlocking concrete pavers, aren't designed to be a visible part of your floor design. Their main purpose is to strengthen your floor by providing horizontal resistance to the pavement, helping to maintain the interlock and load-spreading capabilities of the units. You also install these edging variations after laying your floor surface (rather than before, as you do with most other edging types). Metal edging is very durable and designed to curve easily. You simply position the wedge-shaped restraint in place, then nail it through the foundation base using 10-inch (25.4 cm) nails. PVC edging isn't quite as strong as metal, but if your floor won't have to accommodate vehicle traffic, it'll do its job just fine, as long as you're sure to buy PVC edging that's specified for paving and not for landscape edges.

planting in the gaps:
for fragrance

A starter list of aromatic plants that will release their fragrance (and survive) when they're stepped on:

Chamomile (*Chamaemelum nobile*). Lacy leaves, tiny yellow flowers, the scent of apples.

Cranesbill (*Geranium macrorrhizum*). Perennial with pink flowers and highly fragrant leaves.

Creeping Mint (*Mentha requientii*). Bright green leaves and light purple flowers. Creates a mossy effect. Best in partial shade and evenly moist soil. Minty, sage-like scent.

Lemon Thyme (*Thymus citriodorus*). Variegated gold and green leaves and lavender flowers in late spring. Lemon scented.

Snowbank (*Dianthus gratianopolitanus*). Shaggy plant, white flowers, highly perfumed.

them as you would cut stone. You'll still want level string lines as guides, but you have much more leeway in terms of spacing between the pavers.

Whichever approach you're taking, adjust the sand setting bed underneath the pavers, as necessary, to make sure the tops of the pavers are up against the string level. After laying each row, lay a short length of 2 x 4 across the pavers, and tap it to level them. Use a rubber mallet to level individual pavers, if necessary. Always kneel in the sand behind where you're

BELOW **Concrete pavers do a good job of imitating bluestone in this downtown patio garden.**

RIGHT The muted, natural shade of these concrete paving blocks helps integrate the floor with the setting.

working, so you won't dislodge the pavers you've just set in place. And check your work occasionally with a level to make sure you're maintaining the slope you established when you graded your site.

Compaction

If you've laid interlocking pavers, before you finish the joints, set the pavers in place firmly by making at least two passes over the entire surface with a power compactor.

Joints

Sprinkle clean, fine, dry sand across the surface of your floor, sweep it into the joints with a stiff push broom, and use a hose to sprinkle the floor lightly with water to settle the sand. Repeat the sweeping-and-watering process until the sand is well packed, the joints are full, and the pavers don't wobble. If you're working with interlocking pavers, before sweeping

sand into the joints and wetting it, vibrate a layer of sand into the joints with the power compactor.

Finishing Work

Clean the surface of your floor with a cleaner specifically made for concrete pavers. After the surface is completely dry, you can spray or roll on a concrete paver sealer to protect the surface, if you like. Use a sealant that is made specifically for concrete pavers, not a general, all-purpose solution. And don't seal pavers around a pool deck; the chemicals can leach into the water.

LEFT **Pavers of various colors and cuts resemble an elaborate tiled floor.**

LOWER LEFT **In some cases, inter-locking pavers that create patterns (like the fan-shaped one shown here) are sold in pre-formed slabs of connected pavers.**

maintenance

Over time, individual pavers may dislodge or settle in too deeply. Use a flat-headed screw driver to remove problem pavers, adjust (and in many cases add to) the sand underneath, then position the pavers back into place. Occasionally, you'll also need to replace washed-out sand in the joints between pavers and do a bit of weeding.

Efflorescence, the same whitish mineral that leaches out of bricks, creating stains or streaks, can also plague concrete pavers. If it doesn't disappear with normal weathering, choose a warm, dry day to wash it off with water and a rag or to brush it away with a stiff, dry brush. In addition, you can reapply sealant over the pavers every two to five years to prevent efflorescence, help the pavers resist other stains, and enhance the color of the pavers.

garden floor traditions

Pebble mosaics, today a popular way to personalize concrete pavers, have been used to decorate floors for thousands of years. The ancient Greeks were among the first to make mosaic floors. Those shown here were created with local stone in 350 B.C. (left) and 250 B.C. (middle). Exquisite designs of pebbles pressed into mortar were also created centuries ago in China and by the Arab civilization of Spain—and by those creating gardens in Renaissance Italy (right).

B E L O W **In this small herb and cutting garden, pavers that simulate cut stone create a casual and practical little floor.**

poured
concrete
floors

Poor concrete, it gets such a bad rap. Probably because most of us think of it as a wide, unimaginative expanse of glaring white, best reserved for city sidewalks and office-park entrance-ways. Think again. When you combine the growing number of ways to texturize, tint, and otherwise treat concrete with its marvelous flexibility (you work with it wet, so it conforms to any design you choose), you've got a sturdy paving material you can customize to suit a wide range of garden settings.

PREVIOUS PAGE **This poured and stamped concrete floor connects to precast stepping stones beyond.**

LEFT The joints in this concrete floor were embedded with brick to add interest—and connect it visually with the path beyond.

LOWER LEFT The jointing in this poured-concrete terrace adds to the design. Precast pavers set in turf carry the floor into the yard.

special tools & supplies

Concrete sets up quickly. Prior to starting to work, make sure you have everything you need, so you don't spend precious time searching for tools.

- Heavy gloves

- Rubber boots

- Power compactor

- Rectangular concrete trowel

- Edger (also called an edging trowel, for cutting a rounded edge between the concrete and the form)

- Groover or jointer (for cutting smooth, straight control joints in the floor to prevent cracking)

- Bull float or darby float (These tools smooth out depressions or ridges after you've roughly leveled the cement with a screed. The bull float has a long handle for larger jobs; the darby is best for smaller jobs.)

the good news and the bad news

A concrete floor is one of the most durable types you can install; a well-constructed concrete slab can last up to 30 years, which is exactly the problem if you change your mind once your floor is in place. Altering your design will probably require breaking the floor to pieces and starting over. Concrete also sets up quickly, so there's little time for tweaking your design once you've started to pour.

▪ Wood float (optional) (for giving your floor a rougher finish to improve its traction)

▪ Contractor-quality wheelbarrow (if you are doing the mixing yourself)

▪ Hammer, nails, stakes, and 2 x 4 lumber for constructing forms

▪ Expansion material for filling control joints (You can buy either asphalt-impregnated felt or ½-inch [1.3 cm] molded fiber at home-improvement stores.)

▪ Plastic sheeting or tarp to cover the slab during the curing process (in case of rain).

design options

Because this most durable of paving options is the only one that is soft and flowing when you lay it, you can easily wrap it around a fountain, wind it along the curved edge of a pond, or adapt it to the shape of your space in nearly any other way.

You can also alter the color and texture, whether you want your floor to blend naturally with other landscaping elements, provide a dramatic contrast, or resemble some other paving material altogether. Both tinting agents (available in powder form) and texturizing materials such as decorative gravel will alter the concrete before you pour it. Once you've poured your floor, you can stamp or stencil the still-wet surface with textured patterns to give it the appearance of cobblestone, brick, or other paving materials, or you can embed the surface with anything from stones, seashells, and cut glass to tile fragments and leaves. Various finishing

ABOVE **Here, tinted and stamped concrete takes on the look of stone.**

tools, from stiff brooms to specialized floats, will also alter the surface of your poured floor. Or, wait until the floor has cured, and you can embellish it with concrete stains and paints.

Often, the trick to making concrete look less utilitarian is to use it sparingly and combine it with other materials, from bands of brick to randomly embedded pavers. Decorative edging can also add interest to a concrete floor in danger of seeming static.

quick-glance glossary

The terms concrete and cement fly about interchangeably (with mortar tossed in every now and then, too). It can all be confusing to newcomers who need to know the difference. Here's how the definitions break down.

Cement: Also called Portland cement, this is the limey powder you combine with water and aggregate (sand and/or gravel) to create a durable surface. Premixed cement is Portland cement already mixed with aggregate; it's usually sold by the bag. With premixed cement, you simply add the water.

Concrete: When the cement mixture hardens, it forms concrete.

Mortar: Use a slightly different recipe of cement, aggregate, and water, and you create this mixture that is used as a bonding agent to lay brick, tile, and stone.

installation

The process for installing a concrete floor and pouring a concrete foundation as a firm base for another paving material is essentially the same. You can follow the process below for either situation. If you're simply pouring a foundation, you won't need to finish the surface. However, you will need to dig your foundation deep enough so that there's space to add a setting bed and your pavers on top of the concrete.

ABOVE AND FACING PAGE
Poured concrete is ideal for floors with layouts that flow rather than adhere to straight lines and careful corners. Here, the surfaces have been stamped.

Foundation

Clear and grade your site, and mark your floor layout as described in Chapter 4, page 38, placing your marking material about 1½ inches (3.8 cm) outside of where you want your floor's concrete edge, to allow enough room for wooden forms. Remove the sod, excavate the foundation, and compact the subgrade well, making sure it's free of tree roots, large rocks, and any other matter.

For a concrete floor, your foundation should be deep enough to accommodate 2 to 4 inches (5.1 to 10.2 cm) of crushed rock and 3 inches (7.6 cm) of concrete. (You'll actually pour 4 inches [10.2 cm] of concrete, but the final inch will sit above ground level.) If you're pouring a concrete

ABOVE **You can tint your wet cement before pouring it or paint or stain your cured concrete floor.**

with the surface of your floor, will absorb any fluctuation in the concrete from temperature changes and will help prevent cracking.

About the Foundation's Crushed Rock

◾ Crushed rock as the first layer of your foundation makes your floor stronger and minimizes settling and cracking. However, if you have a dry, solid subgrade that is not clay, you can eliminate the crushed-rock layer without tremendous risk if your floor won't have to accommodate vehicles.

◾ If your soil drains poorly, err on the high side of the range for crushed rock, adding 3 to 4 inches (7.6 to 10.2 cm).

◾ If your floor will have to accommodate vehicles as well as people, increase the amount of crushed rock in the foundation to 6 inches (15.2 cm).

Forms

Wooden forms, typically made by setting 2 x 4 lumber vertically into the ground, hold the concrete in place until it dries. Once the concrete is set, you can do one of three things: rip out the forms, cover them with dirt or sod, or use them as decorative edging.

1 Begin by pounding 12-inch (30.5 cm) wooden stakes into the ground, leaving the tops of the stakes 1 inch (2.5 cm) above the ground. Place the stakes every 3 or 4 feet (.9 or 1.2 m).

2 Use double-headed nails (which will be easy to pull out later) to nail the forms to the stakes (figure 1). Nail from

foundation for another paving material (rather than a concrete floor), increase the depth of your excavation, so you have room for your paving material on top of the concrete.

Along any area where the floor you're building will abut a foundation wall or existing concrete, install asphalt-impregnated expansion joints or ½-inch (1.3 cm) molded fiber, extending down the entire depth of the foundation. These strips, which you set in place so they'll be flush

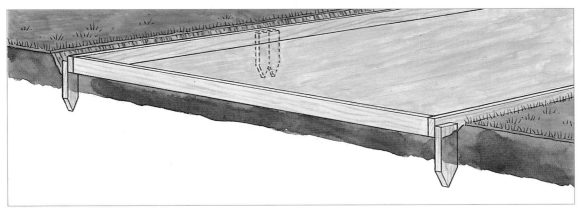

FIGURE 1 **Nail form boards to the stakes.**

the outside of the stakes through the forms (again, this makes it easier to pull out the nails later). As you work, make sure the forms maintain the slope you established when you graded your site. (To protect forms that you want to use as decorative edging when your floor is finished, cover the top edges of the wood with masking tape. If you plan to leave the forms in place and cover them when your floor is finished, use cedar or redwood stakes, and position the stakes and the forms 1 inch [2.5 cm] below the ground rather than above it.)

If the floor you're building features curved edges, use 3½-inch-wide (8.9 cm) hardwood that is ¼ inch (6 mm) thick for your forms. Nail one end of the board to a stake, curve it to the shape you want, cut it, and nail the other end to another stake. You may need to cut slits that go halfway through the board every inch (2.5 cm) or so to help the wood bend.

Mixing the Cement

Premixed bags of cement have everything you need but water, but they're more expensive and primarily suitable for very

let someone else do the mixing

For quantities greater than 1 cubic yard (.76 cubic m), you may want to have a concrete supplier mix the cement for you, deliver it to your site, and pour it directly from the truck to your floor, using a swinging chute. Keep in mind that this option may include unexpected costs (for pumping the cement to the pour area if it's not reachable by a large truck, for example) and added complications (such as ruts from the delivery truck on your lawn). On the other hand, it will save you tremendous time and labor and will reduce the chance for mixing error.

small jobs. In most cases, you'll need Portland cement and aggregate (sand and gravel) that you'll mix together yourself in a wheelbarrow or a large plastic tub.

A good mix for a concrete floor is 1 part Portland cement, 2½ parts clean sand (not mason's sand or ocean sand; the salt will prevent proper curing), 2¾ parts clean, washed gravel (ranging from ¼ to 1 inch [6 mm to 2.5 cm] in size), and ½ part clean, potable water. The proportions may vary depending on where you live and the dampness of your sand; it's a good idea to also ask for advice on proportions from a local concrete supplier. Getting the right mix of ingredients is critical. If your cement mixture is too watery, your concrete will be weak and prone to cracking. If it's too dry, it will be hard to spread evenly, and you could end up with air pockets as a result.

When mixing cement for use in colder climates, you'll want to also include an additive that creates evenly distributed tiny bubbles in the mix. The enhanced mixture, called air-entrained cement, hardens into concrete that better withstands the expansion of freezing. Air-entrained cement must be mixed with a power mixer, rather than by hand. You can order it already mixed from a ready-mix supplier or add an air-entraining admixture to regular cement and mix it with a rented power mixer.

It's always a good idea to mix a small batch of your cement and test it before you pour your floor. When you spread it out with a trowel, the trowel should leave a smooth, wet surface in the cement. If water puddles where your trowel was, the mix needs more dry cement. If the mix is rough and crumbly, carefully and slowly add more water. (The water content of the sand and your area's humidity levels will also affect the moisture of your mixed cement.) A good mixture should feel smooth and creamy, but not soupy or crumbly.

Reinforcement

Adding reinforcement to the foundation in the form of wire mesh or steel rebar isn't necessary for small floors in a residential setting, as long as your cement mix includes strengthening fibers. Most concrete manufacturers are now adding fiberglass to their mix as a strengthener and a replacement for the reinforcing. You can

FIGURE 2 **Screed the wet cement.**

also buy bags of fiberglass from concrete-supply stores. If you're ordering your cement already mixed, specify that the supplier add fiberglass.

Pouring the Floor

When pouring your floor, work in small sections of 3 or 4 feet (.9 or 1.2 m) at a time, completing all the steps listed before you move on to another section.

1   Lightly moisten the forms with a hose.

2   Pour the cement in small patches throughout the section rather than dumping large piles and then dragging it long distances with a rake. Rake the cement to roughly level, using a hard rake (not a leaf rake). If you have your cement delivered, make sure you pour it within 90 minutes of the time it was loaded in the truck. After pouring, move a shovel or hoe up and down in the mixture to remove air bubbles, especially near the edges, but be careful not to overwork it.

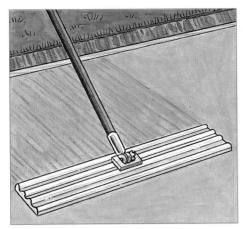

FIGURES 3 & 4 **Use either a bull float (top) or a darby float (bottom) to smooth the surface.**

ABOVE AND LEFT **Pieces of this floor, such as the central green circle, were poured in place with pigmented concrete, then surrounded by precast concrete pavers. Pavers set on end create the floor's edging. The design complement's the home's art deco interior.**

3 With the help of a partner, screed or level the raked cement with a 2 x 4 board that's long enough to rest on the forms on both sides of the floor. Shimmy the screed horizontally across the slab twice (figure 2). Screeding the cement is the first stage of leveling it.

4 Use either the bull float or the darby float to further smooth the surface and push the larger aggregate pieces to the bottom of the slab (figures 3 and 4). Push the float away from you with the front edge slightly raised, and then pull it back again with the blade lying flat. Continue this

FIGURE 5 **Edge the perimeter of the floor.**

FIGURE 6 **Create grooves along the surface to prevent cracking.**

ABOVE **Concrete floors are stable enough that they don't require edging, though you can choose to add it for aesthetic appeal.**

process until water stops rising to the surface. Don't overwork the cement, though, or you'll bring too much fine material to the surface, which makes it weaker.

5 When there is no water visible on the surface, begin edging the perimeter of the floor, moving the edger along the surface with the front tilted up slightly, so it glides smoothly (figure 5).

6 Use the groover or jointer to create grooves along the surface at regular intervals to prevent cracking. Guide the tool against a long plank (figure 6). If you like, the grooves can be integral to the sur-

face design of your floor. A good rule of thumb is to place your grooves the same distance apart as your floor is wide. For floors that are wider than 10 feet (3 m), run a joint down the center of the floor, as well. Control joints should run about 1 inch (2.5 cm) deep for a 4-inch-deep (10.2 cm) floor or 1½ inches (3.8 cm) deep for a 6-inch-deep (15.2 cm) floor (such as a driveway). (If you like, you can cut your joints in later with a circular saw.)

---

tip

Don't plan to pour cement unless the air temperature is at least 40 °F (4 °C) at the coldest part of the day. You'll have the best luck if you install your floor when you expect a month or two of weather in that range or warmer. The temperature will help your floor cure and dry properly.

If you're pouring a concrete foundation for another paving material, you can stop at this point, cover the foundation with a sheet of polyethylene plastic, and let the concrete cure for a week, then add a setting bed and your pavers.

If you're creating a concrete floor, move on to finishing it.

finishing the floor

1 Texturize your surface, so your floor will have some traction and be skid resistant. A wood float will give you a rough surface. So will sweeping a stiff broom across the floor surface. (Be sure not to use a steel float, though; it will create a surface that's too slick.) Now is also the time to enhance your floor by stamping, stenciling, or embedding the surface (see Enhancing the Surface, below). If you're adding quite a bit of texturizing surface decoration, you don't need to texturize the surface with a float or a broom beforehand.

2 Cover your floor with a sheet of polyethylene plastic for a week to hold in the moisture and prevent it from drying too quickly. This curing process allows the concrete to bond properly.

3 Two days after removing the plastic, you can pull off the form boards. Don't walk on the floor for four days after removing the plastic, and don't drive on it for seven days.

4 Backfill any areas around the edge of the floor that might be tripping hazards, and add plantings along the edges, if you like.

garden floor traditions

The Romans were the first to use an artificial paving material similar to today's concrete (for building all those roads, of course). The concept traveled, as did the idea of pressing pebbles and other materials into the concrete to reinforce and decorate both indoor and outdoor concrete floors. This courtyard at an Arabian mosque in Cordoba, Spain, which features a floor of concrete embedded with pebbles, was built between the 9th and 12th centuries.

enhancing the surface

Once your floor is poured, you have about an hour to work on the surface before the concrete is too stiff. You can add a retardant to the concrete mix to slow the hardening process. Even so, if you're adding an intricate surface design (a mosaic, for example), you'll probably want to pour and complete only small sections of your floor at a time.

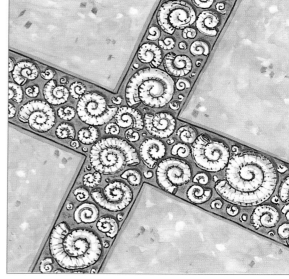

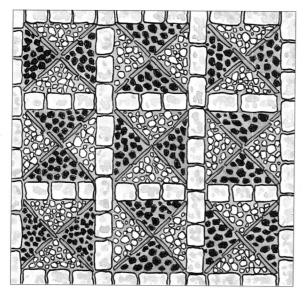

Concrete embedded with glazed tiles, brick, and tile shards (UPPER LEFT); lines of stone paving blocks and black and white pebbles (BOTTOM); and shells in the joints between pavers (UPPER RIGHT)

Embedding Materials

Glazed tiles, pottery shards, interesting found objects (see the horseshoe embedding on page 142), colored glass, leaves, and countless other materials can personalize the surface of your concrete floor, whether you place the pieces randomly, position them inside decorative edges, or create an elaborate mosaic. The basics for embedding are the same; you simply change the material and design to suit your style.

1 Pour only as much wet cement as you can embed in about an hour (or less if the weather is hot and dry). After that time, it will be too hard to work with. You may even want to add a retardant, which you can buy at a hardware store, to slow the cement's hardening.

2 With your mapped-out design and the objects to be embedded close at hand, slip on some rubber gloves and press the pieces in place. You may want to rest a long, sturdy board across the forms on either side of your floor, so you can kneel on it as you work.

3 After you finish a section, lay a thin piece of plywood over the embedded surface and apply light pressure to firmly embed the objects, tamping them to about even with the concrete.

4 When the concrete is hard, typically after about 36 to 48 hours, sweep the embedded surface clean with a stiff broom.

Coloring the Concrete

Concrete paints and stains are both available at home improvement stores. The paint (choose water-based latex paint) simply coats the surface, while the stain infiltrates the concrete. Check the manufacturer's instructions on whether you need to apply a primer first. Typically, you won't, but if your concrete floor is freshly installed, make sure it's completely cured before you apply the paint or stain. You may also need to etch the surface first with muriatic acid to roughen it up. If your concrete floor has been in place for awhile, wash it and let it dry completely before adding color. Finally, look for an inconspicuous spot where you can test the paint or stain you've chosen to make sure it's what you had in mind before you bathe your floor in it. You may need to apply several coats of your coloring agent to achieve the look you want. Both paint and stain will weather over time, so you'll have to freshen the color occasionally.

Stamping

Stamping concrete floors is becoming an increasingly popular technique. Stamps come in patterns ranging from brick and tile to quarried stone, and they're often used in conjunction with coloring agents to create a quite natural look. Most home landscapers hire a contractor with imprinting tools to help with the stamping, which can be a complex process, especially on a large floor.

TOP **Hand-painted concrete**

BOTTOM **A simple stamping job, this pigmented concrete was stamped with the frond of a yucca plant.**

On a much simpler level, you can stamp small sections with purchased or home-made stamps that make impressions of everything from animal tracks to letters of the alphabet.

Texturizing

Different floats and brooms can give the surface of your concrete floor various subtle textures, but if you want something more dramatic, add extra aggregate to your cement mix, then expose it. For best effect, use an aggregate (decorative pebbles, for example) that contrasts in color with the concrete. Once you've finished the wet surface of your floor with a float, let it dry for about 6 hours, then remove a thin layer of concrete with a stiff-bristled brush followed by a fine spray of water, until the aggregate is exposed. (Careful not to expose too much, though. About two-thirds of each piece of aggregate should remain embedded.) Let your floor set for another 36 to 48 hours, then clean any remaining concrete from the aggregate with a high-pressure water jet.

ABOVE **An aggregate of pea gravel was added to this pigmented mix, then exposed.**

UPPER LEFT **Poured concrete featuring exposed aggregate and embedded with a design of precast pavers**

LOWER LEFT **Quartzite aggregate was added to this concrete before it was poured to give it a sparkling effect. It was finished with a broom.**

Another way to achieve a similar look is to sprinkle small stones into the surface of the concrete before it dries. In warm climates that don't experience winter freezes, you can also create a pitted surface by evenly scattering ordinary rock salt across the surface of your wet concrete, using about 3 to 6 pounds (1.4 to 2.7 kg) of salt per 200 square feet (18 square m) of surface area. Roll a piece of plastic pipe over the salt to embed it in the concrete, allow the concrete to cure for seven days, then wash and brush the surface.

maintenance

Though concrete floors need very little care and attention, you can do a few things to keep yours in shape.

▪ Protect your new floor from draining water (the kind that might run out of downspouts).

▪ Don't use salt or other de-icers during the first winter. After that, use de-icers that contain only sodium chloride or calcium chloride.

▪ Water-repellent sealers can help reduce damage from freeze-thaw cycles and from salt, but some may slightly darken your floor. Follow your sealer's instructions regarding how long to wait after the concrete has been poured before you can seal it. Most sealers are effective for about two years.

exposing decorative aggregate

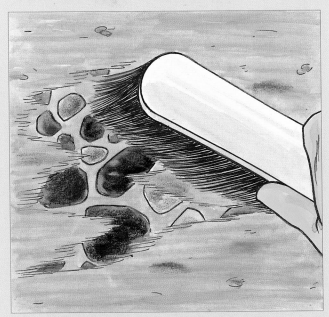

Remove a thin layer of concrete to expose about one-third of the aggregate.

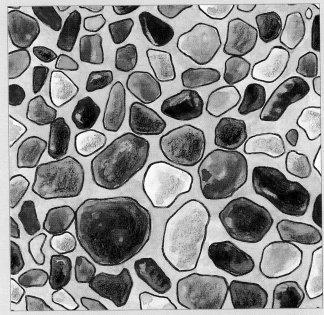

After another 36 to 48 hours, clean any remaining concrete residue with a high-pressure water jet.

floors
of recycled & nontraditional materials

Some gardens—and, more to the point, some gardeners—simply aren't cut out for tidy rows of new, neatly mortared bricks or perfectly molded concrete pavers. If tried and true approaches have always been a bit too predictable for you, you've probably got your suspicions that standard paving materials are only a starting point. Here's a sampling of one-of-a-kind floors—from funky to modern to highly personalized—that proves you're exactly right.

PREVIOUS PAGE These recycled railroad tracks and ties were laid on compacted gravel over compacted earth. (Note: One of the reasons wooden railroad ties are available for recycling is that they've been treated with creosote to keep them from rotting. This gooey, tar-like substance can stain clothes. And it makes the ties best for floors that don't incorporate ground cover; it can be toxic to plants.)

RIGHT Manhole covers and machinery parts in a setting bed of mulch create a quirky garden floor outside an artist's warehouse studio.

BELOW A millstone whose days of grinding grain are long gone creates a focal point in a tiny brick terrace.

industrial cast-offs

Gone is the time when recycling meant grudgingly making do with already used leftovers. Today, salvage yards and flea markets have become hot shopping spots, as more and more of us seek out pieces that feature the nicks, chips, and other imperfections that prove they've got some history.

recycled paving

Ironic, but often you can end up with great paving material by snatching up what someone else decides is no longer good enough.

ABOVE **An interesting arrangement of sidewalk shards creates a center-piece in a brick and con-crete patio.**

LEFT AND BELOW **When the city of Easley, South Carolina, ripped out its streets' granite curb-stones, the landscapers at J. Dabney Peeples Design Associates, Inc., trans-formed the decades-old ma-terial into their firm's front entranceway.**

LEFT **Pine needles gathered on site make this cozy seating area look all the more relaxing.**

natural materials

Some of the most obvious materials you can recycle into paving for your floor are those that already make themselves comfortably at home in your yard: pine needles, bark mulches, leaves, and the like. They create soft, welcoming surfaces that blend seamlessly with their surroundings. They're also some of the easiest and least expensive materials to work with.

Recycled wood rounds set in sand or mortar create a charmingly rustic floor. Cut the rounds with a chain saw (usually 8 to 10 inches [20.3 to 25.4 cm] thick), let them dry out, then soak them in a penetrating wood preservative before laying them. One word of caution: it's best to attempt this version of rustic charm in dry areas and on properly draining soil only. In soggy soil, even treated wood rounds will eventually become covered with moss, making for an extremely slippery surface.

If your soil drains well, you can probably get away with simply clearing the surface you've marked out for your floor, adding some simple edging, and spreading on several inches of your paving layer (did we mention that these are casual floors?). For better protection against a mud-filled floor after a heavy rain, go ahead and dig a foundation 4 to 6 inches (10.2 to 15.2 cm) deep and fill it with compacted crushed rock (see page 42 for details), then spread on your surface layer. You'll likely need to replenish natural paving materials frequently (at least once a year) as they pack down and decompose. Natural-material floors also require a bit of weeding now and then.

nontraditional
materials

Just as interesting as cleverly recycling a material is choosing a paving material that's entirely unexpected. Place something people typically associate with manufacturing plants beneath garden benches and pots of flowers, and your worries about coming up with good conversation starters for your garden parties are over.

ABOVE **In these two city gardens, floors of industrial grating blend well with the contemporary, urban setting. In one, the grating is placed on crushed stone and edged with painted timbers (and topped with commercial-grade mixing bowls as planters). In the other, the grating is settled into black lava rock.**

RIGHT **Embedding concrete is one of the most effective paving techniques for adding originality to an outdoor floor. A household of horse lovers used the technique to link their porch floor with the one in the room just beyond. (For details on embedding concrete, see page 132.)**

personalized paving

Of course, the best way to create a garden floor that defies standard classification is to pave it with something all your own.

garden floor traditions

Where better to find fabulous pieces to recycle than a region loaded with artifacts? This entranceway to the Acropolis in Athens, Greece, was laid with open joints on gravel using remnant pieces of marble from the structure itself.

LEFT **With a nod to the notion that anything goes when you're adding personality to your garden, the creators of this small, informal seating area wedged chunks of their recently removed bathroom tile in among more traditional paving units.**

acknowledgments

Special thanks to:

J. Dabney Peeples, Arthur Campbell, Graham A. Kimak, and many of the fine clients of J. Dabney Peeples Design Associates, Inc., Easley, South Carolina. All spent a great deal of time taking us through their gardens, our notepads and cameras in tow.

John Thelen of Landmark Landscapes, Swannanoa, North Carolina, who contributed expertise, tools, and a whole lot of physical labor to create the book's how-to photographs. Thanks also to his clients, Stuart and Jean McLennan, also of Swannanoa, who allowed us to dig up their yard.

Dr. Arnold R. Alanen and his colleague, Doug Hadley, who assisted with historic imagery and information. Dr. Alanen is a professor in the department of landscape architecture at the University of Wisconsin-Madison, where he has taught landscape history and landscape preservation courses for more than twenty-five years. He is the recipient of several awards for his research work, including two recent citations from the American Society of Landscape Architects for his studies of national park cultural landscapes in Alaska and Michigan. He is the co-editor of the book *Preserving Cultural Landscapes in America* (Johns Hopkins University Press, 2000).

The "Garden Femmes": Dana Irwin (Lark Books art director) and Cindy Burda, Janice Eaton Kilby, and Kathy Sheldon (Lark Books editors). These collaborators extraordinaire, while busy with their own books, somehow found time to help locate and style a number of the shots in this one.

Veronika Alice Gunter, assistant editor, whose extraordinary organizational abilities are surpassed only by her patience and diplomacy. This book would not have been possible without her.

And thanks especially Mary Weber, the book's consultant. Her expert technical knowledge, keen eye for detail, enthusiastic interest in the subject, and unfailing good humor (often in the face of avalanches of deadlines) made her an exceptional partner in this project.

photo credits

Much thanks to the landscape architects and others who submitted photography for this book:

Dr. Arnold Alanen and Doug Hadley, University of Wisconsin: pages 55, 85, 95 (bottom), 107, 131

Arbor Engineering, Greenville, SC; Tom Keith, architect: pages 11 (middle), 100 (top)

Bomanite, Madera, CA; Dino Tom, photographer: pages 17, 120-121, 123, 124, 125, 126, 130

Brick Industry Association, Reston, VA: pages 13 (top), 19 (bottom of column), 56

Broussard Associates Landscape Architects, Clovis, CA; Terry Broussard, ASLA, architect; Larry Falke, photographer: pages 86-87, 122 (bottom)

J. Dabney Peeples Design Associates, Inc., Easley, SC; Graham A. Kimak, photographer: pages 22 (top), 23 (middle of column), 105 (top), 139 (bottom left and right)

Daniel's Landscaping, Campbellsport, WI; Daniel Stukenberg, architect/photographer: pages 70-71

Hanover Architectural Products, Hanover, PA: pages 114, 117, 118

Kellogg Landscape Architecture Construction, Inc., Bastrop, TX; Sandra Chipley Kellogg, architect and photographer: page 90 (bottom)

Graham A. Kimak, Greenville, SC; landscape designer/photographer: page 140 (top)

Landplan Studio, Fair Lawn, NJ; Dennis Muhr, architect/photographer: page 105 (bottom)

Missouri Botanical Gardens, St. Louis, MO; Jack Jennings, photographer: pages 20-21 (bottom), 77 (upper left)

Signe Nielsen Landscape Architect, P.C., New York, NY; Signe Nielsen, architect/photographer: pages 22 (middle of column), 67, 71, 76, 77 (bottom row), 89, 100 (bottom), 104, 110 (top), 111 (top and bottom), 119 (top row), 129, 133, 134 (top right and bottom), 136-137, 141 (top left), 142 (bottom right)

Dana Schock and Associates, Sudbury, MA; Dana Schock, ASLA, architect/photographer: cover, pages 11 (top), 19 (bottom left), 54

SJYDesign, Oakland, CA; Steven J. Young, architect; Michelle Burke, photographer: pages 12, 72

Ken Smith, New York, NY, architect: page 141 (right top and bottom)

Mary Smith Associates, P.C., Quincy, MA; Mary Smith architect/photographer: page 83 (top)

Tile Heritage Foundation, Healdsburg, CA; Joseph Taylor, photographer: page 66

Additional photography credits:

Chandoha Photography, Annandale, NJ: pages 79, 84 (bottom)

Derek Fell's Horticultural Picture Library, Gardenville, PA: pages 77 (upper right), 92 (top), 134 (top left), 138 (bottom), 140 (bottom)

Thom Gaines, Asheville, NC: pages 18, 22 (bottom of column), 25 (bottom of column), 110 (middle and botton), 111 (middle)

Dana Irwin, Asheville, NC: page 142 (top)

Dency Kane, New York, NY: pages 62, 78, 101, 103

Janice Eaton Kilby, Asheville, NC: page 142 (bottom left)

Susan L'Hommedieu, Hudson, OH: page 139 (top)

Charles Mann Photography, Santa Fe, NM: pages 11 (bottom), 53, 68, 69, 80-81, 82, 91, 113 (top), 122 (top)

Jerry Pavia Photography, Bonners Ferry, ID: pages 2-3, 5, 8, 9, 14 (top), 15, 20 (top), 22, 24, 25 (top), 26 (top), 51, 60, 64-65, 73, 94, 95 (top), 98-99, 108-109

James Haig Streeter, San Francisco, CA: pages 63, 80

continued on next page

continued from previous page

We also want to acknowledge several artisans whose work is showcased in the book:

Circle of Stone, Haywood County, NC; David Reed, stonemason: page 96

Gardensphere, Sugar Grove, NC; Robbie Oates, stonemason: pages 34 (bottom), 92 (bottom)

Michael Huba, Albany, NY; artist/photographer: page 112

Landscape Gardeners, Biltmore Forest, NC; Art Garst, landscape designer: page 16

Finally, special thanks to those who allowed us to photograph their gardens:

Roger Bakeman, Atlanta, GA: page 113 (bottom)

Trena and Ed Parker, Biltmore Forest, NC: page 61

"Carlsbad" home of Hazel and Paul Sanger, Highlands, NC: page 6

Asheville, NC:

John Cram: page 59

Elizabeth Eve: page 57

Hedy Fischer and Randy Shull: page 97

Dr. Peter and Jasmin Gentling: page 34 (top)

Andrew Glasgow: pages 116, 116-117

Mary Johnson: pages 14 (bottom), 82-83

William and Barbara Lewin: page 18

Christopher Mello: page 138 (top)

Heather Spencer and Charles Murray: pages 12-13 (bottom)

Greenville and Easley, SC:

Jack and Joyce Clarkson, Easley, SC: pages 102, 106

Michael and Kathy Evans, Greenville, SC: pages 23 (top), 119 (bottom)

Janice and Bill Hagler, Greenville, SC: page 90 (top)

Porter and Ann Roe Rose, Greenville, SC: pages 74-75, 88

index